CO. Mobilgas
GILBERT
RIO GRANDE
AUTO REPAIRING
GARAGE
GILBERT, ARIZ.—No.1

Mercy Gilbert Medical Center

A member of CHW

Mercy Gilbert Medical Center sponsored the publication of this pictorial history of Gilbert, Arizona. We thank them and honor them as we present their great work in and for our community.

RENDERING OF MERCY GILBERT MEDICAL CENTER

IN MARCH OF 2004, STUDENTS AT THE BRAND NEW SPECTRUM ELEMENTARY SCHOOL WERE INVITED TO LINE UP ON THE OUTLINE OF THE HOSPITAL, MARKED IN THE OTHERWISE UNDISTURBED ALFALFA FIELD. A HELICOPTER FLEW OVERHEAD TO TAKE A PICTURE OF THE FUTURE OF GILBERT HEALTHCARE AS OUTLINED BY GILBERT'S FUTURE LEADERS.

Main Street, Gilbert, Arizona

THE
DONNING COMPANY
PUBLISHERS

GILBERT
ARIZONA

From Cowboys and Sodbusters to a Mega-Residential Community

Dale C. Hallock

The Donning Company Publishers
184 Business Park Drive, Suite 206
Virginia Beach, VA 23462

Steve Mull, General Manager
Barbara Buchanan, Office Manager
Wendy Nelson, Editor
Mellanie Denny, Graphic Designer
Derek Eley, Imaging Artist
Debby Dowell, Project Research Coordinator
Scott Rule, Director of Marketing
Tonya Hannink, Marketing Coordinator

Carey Southwell, Project Director

Library of Congress Cataloging-in-Publication Data

Hallock, Dale C., 1935-
Gilbert, Arizona: from cowboys and sodbusters to a mega-residential community /
by Dale C. Hallock.
p. cm.
ISBN 978-1-57864-440-7 (hard cover : alk. paper)
1. Gilbert (Ariz.)--History. 2. Gilbert (Ariz.)--History--Pictorial works. 3. Gilbert (Ariz.)--Economic conditions. 4. Gilbert (Ariz.)--Social conditions.
I. Title.
F819.G46H35 2007
979.1'73--dc22

2007022368

Printed in the United States of America
at Walsworth Publishing Company

Contents

Foreword 6

Acknowledgments 7

Introduction 8

I Cowboys and Sodbusters 10

Cowboys • Homestead Entries • Farmers • Depot

II Railroad 18

Murphy's Railroad • Railroad in 1903 • Mining in Kelvin Area • Depot Built in 1905 • Shipping in Gilbert • Bank of Gilbert • Early Homes

III Farming 30

Early Farming • Farm Equipment • Early Crops • Dams • Canals

IV Schools 50

1900 School • 1909 School • 1913 Elementary School • 1920 High School • Modern Schools

V Gilbert 58

William M. "Bobby" Gilbert • Early Businesses • First Subdivisions • First World War • Hay Shipping Center of the World
Churches • 1920 Town Incorporation • 1925 Water Tower and Early Jail

VI Depression and War 74

Old Downtown • Floods • World War II • Gilbert Servicemen • Gilbert Airport • Police • Fire Protection

VII Infrastructure 104

1950s through 1980s • Streets Paved • Sewer System • Gilbert Days • Strip Annexation • New Subdivisions

VIII New Growth 114

New Subdivisions • Street Improvements • Downtown Becomes Old Town • Modern Churches • New Schools • New Town Hall

IX Massive Growth 128

City Complex Addition • Modern Subdivision • New Apartment Buildings • Freeway • New Shopping Centers • Modern Parks

X Hospital 140

Mercy Gilbert Medical Center

About the Author 144

Foreword

When the opportunity to produce the first pictorial history of Gilbert was presented to the Gilbert Historical Society, it was an easy decision to select the writer of the book. Dale Hallock, board member of the historical society, had been writing and researching for many years, intending to write a very detailed and comprehensive history of our town. He was more than willing to take all the material he had gathered and put excerpts of it into a pictorial history book.

Anyone who has been in Gilbert for any length of time knows Dale Hallock. Dale came to Gilbert when he was sixteen months old. He went to school here and was the mayor of the town from July 1971 to July 1976. During his tenure as mayor, he and the Town Council annexed approximately fifty-three square miles (thirty-five thousand acres) in Gilbert that would have been taken over by neighboring towns. Without this effort, Gilbert would have continued to be about two square miles in size, with a population of approximately two thousand people (1,971 in 1970). It's unlikely that a book like this would have been written or that the history of the town would have generated much interest prior to that time.

As one of the fastest-growing communities in the country, Gilbert's unprecedented growth makes history happen each and every day. But that wasn't always true. Since its incorporation in 1920 with five hundred people, Gilbert's population stayed pretty stagnant until this strip annexation took place in the mid-'70s. By 1980, the population was 5,746 and growing fast. By mid-2007, we are at almost 200,000 residents. Incredible! That is definitely a story in itself, and one that we hope to tell in this book.

We would especially like to thank Catholic Healthcare West/Mercy Gilbert Medical Center for sponsoring this book. Without their partnership on this project, it couldn't have happened. On behalf of the Gilbert Historical Society, it is our hope that whether you are one of the new residents of town, one of the dwindling natives, or just someone interested in the history of the area, you will find this book to be full of rich information documented with photographs that together tell the story of how Gilbert came to be.

Kayla Kolar
Executive Director
Gilbert Historical Museum

Acknowledgments

We wish to thank all those who have assisted in the gathering of pictures, maps, and historical material to create this pictorial history of Gilbert. This project has given us the opportunity to remember items of historical significance that we have forgotten over the years.

A great thank you goes to Mercy Gilbert Medical Center for their sponsorship of this publication. Without their financial assistance, the material would have continued to lie quietly in the archives of the Gilbert Historical Museum or in files in town hall. We have often guessed or assumed we had reliable information, but because of the financial aid from Mercy Gilbert we have been motivated to research and record correct dates and times of historical events.

The Gilbert Historical Society and the Gilbert Historical Museum have furnished most of the material presented in this book and have even more historical artifacts in their collections. Kayla Kolar, the Executive Director of the Gilbert Museum, has been more than an assistant in creating this book—she has been an editor, a source of encouragement, and a powerful force in the completion of the work.

Ann Wilson, a museum volunteer, has spent the past several months scanning pictures and pulling negatives and original pictures to showcase the visual history of our town. Without her efforts, this work would not be available. Marji Scotten, president of the Historical Society, has thrown her support to this mission. Carol Knollmiller provided the chronological approach that has been used in this history. Thank you also to the Gilbert Historical Society Board of Directors.

We acknowledge the Town of Gilbert for all their assistance and support. Sue Roberts of the Public Information Office for the Town of Gilbert has provided copies of ordinances, maps, and additional material to substantiate our history. The town has also provided pictures for our use.

Georganne Hallock and her ancestors (from their personal histories) have also contributed pictures. Suzanne Clevenger provided a number of the pictures of the new subdivisions in Gilbert. Jerry Hyman also gave photographic assistance.

Thanks to Boyd Hughes, who furnished us with a painting of his father, Pat Hughes, one of the early cowboys of Arizona.

Danette Turner provided our community with a great book on the history of the Gilbert Police Department. She helped us by providing pictures from her book, *From Star to Shield,* to use in this work.

Other editorial assistance has been given by M. James Snarr and by another friend, Jack Joyce. Mr. Joyce has read every word of the text and made corrections and suggestions to simplify understanding throughout the book.

There are so many others who have assisted with individual contributions to the history of Gilbert that we simply cannot name them all. Please accept our thanks and grateful appreciation.

Finally, in the process of reviewing the incredible resources we have on hand at the Gilbert Museum, it was clear that the founders of the Gilbert Historical Society are to be honored. People like John and Zelda Freestone, John and Ola Sawyer, John and Delia Allen, Morris and Trudy Cooper, Rose Divelbess, Ruth Gieszl, Ann Pace, Elizabeth Hagren, Ethel Mastin, Otto and Edna Neely, and so many others who created the Gilbert Historical Museum gathered and preserved the artifacts we have today.

Thank you to everyone who has preserved the history of our town.

Introduction

Why write the history of our town?
For my family, Gilbert, Arizona, offered a lifestyle that they and many people in America at that time were seeking. In most family histories of the early settlers who came to Gilbert, it is clear that they, too, were seeking land, freedom and success.

Many of the first settlers who came were cowboys looking for range for their cattle. The Homestead Entry Act was their opportunity to acquire land cheaply. The sodbusters were looking for the same privilege of reasonable land to farm. Both cowboys and farmers began filing on property in the Gilbert area in the 1890s.

Others came to escape the 1917 Depression. Even more came after the stock market crash in 1929 brought on the Great Depression of the 1930s. During this same period, the Dust Bowl drove many from Arkansas, Oklahoma, and Texas to the Gilbert area.

This pictorial review of Gilbert history is about those who found success here and stayed. Everything that is Gilbert today has been built upon the good works of those who came before us and left their mark on our community.

Those early cowboys and sodbusters left more than their gravestones behind them. They started schools, opened businesses, built a bank, and granted a right-of-way for a train line that opened our area to commerce and the world. These early people built a water tower and furnished potable water to residents in our first subdivisions. They paved Main Street and later provided a sewer system. From these very beginnings of Gilbert, we have grown into a mega-residential community of almost 200,000 people.

Our first full-service hospital, Mercy Gilbert Medical Center, has just been completed and adds to the wonderful miracle of modernization that we are privileged to enjoy.

I hope that all readers of this book, whether they are current and former Gilbert residents or have never been to Gilbert at all, gain a greater appreciation of our wonderful community through this text.

Gilbert has gone through many changes and will continue to change. The sad part is that those we have learned of in our early history have already died. There are few people remaining who have a memory of Gilbert dating to 1920, for example. Those that do have a perspective on our history are asked to assist us by recording that information in the Family Library we are maintaining at the Gilbert Historical Museum. Precise information from firsthand knowledge will aid us in having a more detailed history of more recent days. Fifty years from now or beyond, such knowledge will be priceless to future students of Gilbert history.

Dale C. Hallock

GARAGE
GILBERT, ARIZ.

CHAPTER 1

Cowboys and Sodbusters

This chapter contains pictures of some late nineteenth and early twentieth-century Gilbert cowboys and sodbusters.

John Anderson was Gilbert's first homesteader who stayed on the land his family acquired by a homestead patent in 1891. He and his family came west to farm and raise white face cattle. His son, Bill Anderson, carried on the tradition, and even though he also farmed, he truly was a cowboy all his life. The Anderson family had been farmers when they lived in North Dakota and before that in Ontario, Canada. They came to Arizona in 1886. They developed their land into a farm as well as a cattle-feeding operation. John Anderson also served on the Gilbert School Board.

JOHN ANDERSON (1850–1933)

❦ WILLIAM BARKLEY FAMILY, 1886

William Barkley and his son Tex "Gus" Barkley were homesteaders in Gilbert. Not only were they cattlemen, but they were also farmers. The first two elementary schools in Gilbert were erected on lands that the Barkley family homesteaded.

❦ TEX "GUS" BARKLEY

❦ BILL ANDERSON (1881–1946)

Bob Bowen was an early cowboy in Gilbert and remained a cowboy until his death.

These were but a few of those who came to our area to raise cattle on the wild oats and Indian wheat that grew naturally in the desert.

Two of the early farmers to homestead were James Pine and his son Charles Pine, who farmed as soon as they could get water to their land. The Pine homestead patent was filed on July 11, 1896. Charles Pine was one of the early members of the Gilbert School Board in 1913.

Clyde McFrederick also came to Gilbert to be a farmer. He acquired land that had been initially homesteaded by John Cuber in 1892. His son Wayne McFrederick also farmed and taught school.

JAMES PINE, ORIGINAL HOMESTEADER (1839–1926)

CHARLES PINE, SON OF JAMES PINE (1867–1917)

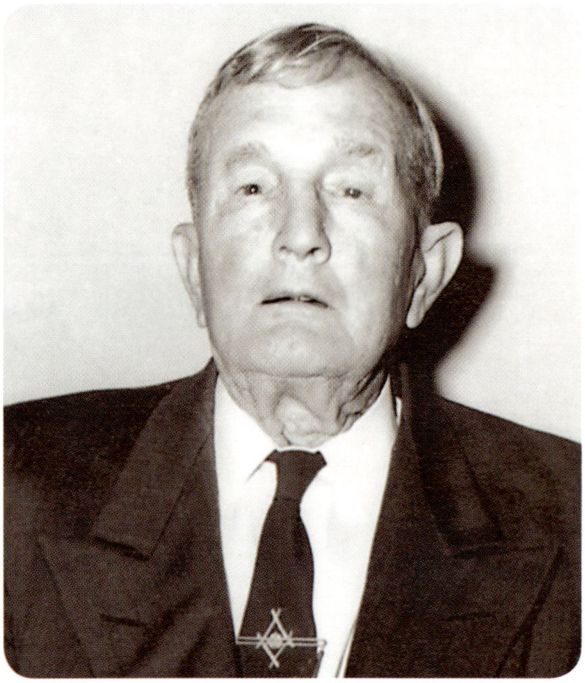

ORSON COOPER (1877–1968)

Orson Cooper came to Arizona as a young boy. He later moved to Gilbert to farm and developed a dairy near Baseline and Cooper Roads. Cooper Road was named for him. His brother Jim became a member of the Arizona House of Representatives and served there for many years. Morris Cooper, another brother, served as Mayor of Gilbert for eight years in the 1960s. Morris and his wife Gertrude, were very involved in the creation of the Gilbert Historical Museum.

Mr. Hubert Sawyer homesteaded land on Val Vista Road in 1908 before going back to Indiana to bring his wife and son to Arizona in 1909. He and his son, John Sawyer, were both active in the education system in Gilbert. Hubert and John both taught school. John served for many years on the Gilbert School Board. Not long after the family arrived in Gilbert, his daughter Elizabeth was born. Elizabeth Sawyer Heagren served as the treasurer of the Gilbert Historical Society for twenty-seven years. She is currently a Trustee Emeritus for the Society.

HUBERT SAWYER (1875–1936)

CHARLES BRASS (1867–1935)

The Charles Brass family came to the Gilbert area to farm in 1901. They later homesteaded land at the corner of Ray Road and Gilbert Road. Ruth Gieszl, one of their grandchildren, still serves as Trustee Emeritus of the Gilbert Historical Society.

Fred Weeks homesteaded land in Gilbert in 1898, and his family has continued to farm and ranch in the Salt River Valley since that time. The Weeks family was better known for their cattle operations in the 1900s.

In chapter five, we will explore more about William M. "Bobby" Gilbert, the namesake of our town. It needs to be noted here that he did homestead the Southeast Quarter of Section 12, Township 1 South, Range 5 East of the Gila and Salt River Base and Meridian on June 10, 1898. This parcel ran from the Western Canal south to Elliot Road and for a half-mile west. His sale of the right-of-way for the Phoenix and Eastern Railroad in 1902 was the fortuitous beginning of Gilbert.

WILLIAM M. "BOBBY" GILBERT (1859–1945)

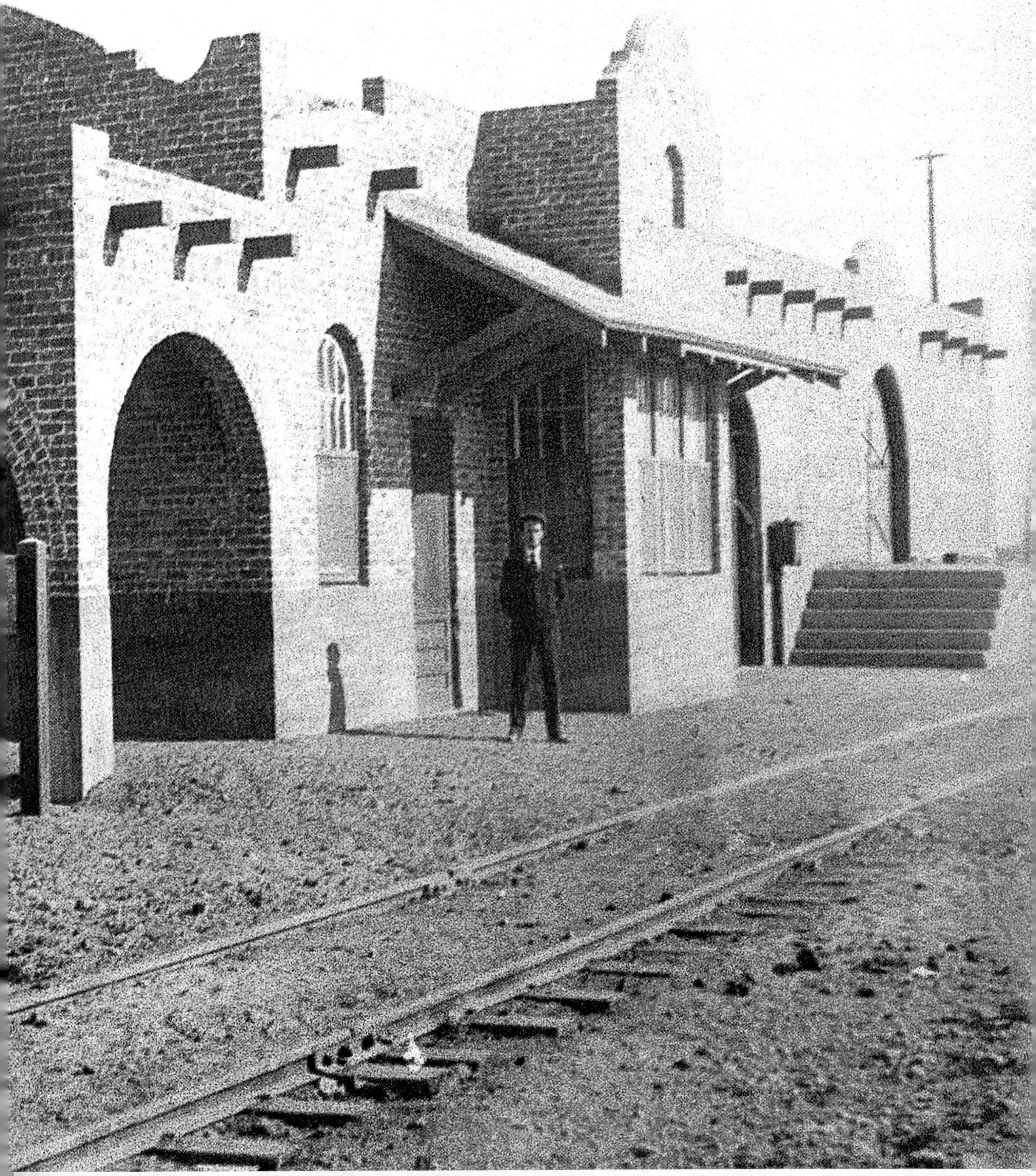

PAT
HUGHES
FROM LIFE -
APRIL 1944 -
GEO.
FREDERICK

After the first citizens arrived in the area later to be known as Gilbert, Arizona, many followed. The Phoenix and Eastern Railroad brought their line through the area in 1903. By 1905, there was a Gilbert Depot on a spur that would become the focal point of our town. Merchants also came to provide services, and our community was born.

It is necessary for us to keep in mind that these original homesteaders, cowboys, and sodbusters laid the foundation for our community. After the first land patents were issued in 1891, they were soon digging ditches, farming, and building homes and barns. The establishment of this community was well underway before the railroad came through our area and actually put Gilbert on the map.

The cowboys and sodbusters were very active in providing the growing town of Gilbert with educational opportunities. Both groups contributed to the establishment of businesses and public services to attend to the basic needs of themselves and their children.

Our ancestors who farmed here used animal power almost exclusively to do the hard work of plowing, planting, and harvesting. The crops could only be raised on the small amount of water available before the Water Reclamation Act. Theodore Roosevelt signed the National Water Reclamation Act on June 17, 1902. Prior to this enactment, the dream of the future water-control system that we now call the Salt River Project was just that, a dream. The dams and canal systems that were put in place in the early 1900s gave Gilbert the foundation to become a great farming community. Since the 1970s, we have become a residential community with more and more residential subdivisions being built in what was our farm town.

The following is an account of Gilbert's own cowboy, William Patton Hughes, who was born in Kentucky in 1877. Pat left home at thirteen and went to Mexico, where he learned the cowboy trade. Pat Hughes was a ranch hand all his life. He worked ranches around Arizona and in Gilbert, including the Starvation Ranch near Winslow, Arizona. The operation was under the famous Hash-Knife Cattle Company.

Pat was also in the 1903 Wild West Rodeo with Annie Oakley and Buffalo Bill that was held in London, England. He told me that Buffalo Bill couldn't "sit a horse." In cowboy parlance, that meant he couldn't ride a horse. After being a part of the Buffalo Bill Wild West Show, Pat returned to the southwest. In Magdalena, New Mexico in 1903, he married Oneta Martin, and they had eight children. Pat's children all attended Gilbert schools.

PAT HUGHES (1877–1955)

This 1944 painting of Pat Hughes was hanging in the Buckhorn Museum at the corner of Recker Road and the Apache Trail (Main Street) in Mesa before I met Pat when I was fifteen. The painting, by George Frederick, details the roughness and simplicity of our cowboy era. Alice Sliger and her husband Ted, the owners of the Buckhorn Museum, were close friends of both Pat Hughes and George Frederick, the painter. When Alice turned one hundred years old in 2006, she decided to close the Buckhorn Museum and to give this painting of Pat Hughes to Boyd and Dorothy Hughes, his son and daughter-in-law. They allowed us to photograph the painting for the Gilbert Historical Museum. The picture of this painting is now included in this pictorial history of Gilbert.

CHAPTER II

Railroad and Other Transportation

The railroad through Gilbert, Arizona was a dream of Frank Murphy, who came to Arizona in 1877. He later incorporated the Phoenix and Eastern Railroad Company on August 31, 1901. Murphy's purpose in building his railroad was to bring copper and gold from the mountains around the Kelvin, Mammoth, Winkleman, Mineral Creek (later called Ray), and Hayden mining towns, all situated along the Gila River. Gold had been found in Mammoth in 1879 on the Hackeny and Aaben claims. In 1903, ninety-six miles of track was laid from Phoenix through the Gilbert area and on to Winkleman.

The line ran from Phoenix through Tempe and on to Mesa, where it turned south. At Baseline Road, the track turned southeasterly in an almost straight line to a point on the north side of the Gila River near Florence. At that point the track met the Gila River, following the river easterly to the great mineral deposits that were already being developed.

With limited water resources, a few of the early farmers were already growing alfalfa in the area. The future Gilbert just happened to lie along the route for the Phoenix and Eastern Railroad.

Man with springwagon. Springs were added for comfort.

Otis Barkley with horse and buggy. Otis was a member of the Barkley pioneer family

The almost straight-line portion of the Phoenix and Eastern was a blessing for Murphy and his railroad, as the land was almost level all the way to the Gila River. The base work from Mesa to Florence was not too difficult for the workers, but they still had to clear, grub, and grade a roadbed with only men and mules. Using scrapers, pick, and shovel, the men moved quickly across the desert. The work went well until they reached the mountains, where they had to tunnel and bridge the Gila River on their way to Kelvin and their mining interests.

After incorporation in 1901, Murphy began to acquire rights-of-way to Kelvin and Winkleman. Murphy dealt with James Pine for a right-of-way, to which Pine agreed. Pine asked that a spur be placed along the track at the next roadway. That road is now called Gilbert Road.

The first right-of-way purchased from Bobby Gilbert was only the usual width of sixty-six feet. Murphy later acquired an additional parcel sixty-seven feet in width to allow for a future sidetrack or spur, and a depot was built in 1905.

HAY BALING. THE FARMERS' SUCCESS WAS GREATLY INCREASED BY RAILROAD TRANSPORTATION.

HEAVY SHIPMENT

Four buggies on the way to the Anderson Ranch. Prior to the railroad there was only one form of transportation.

Gilbert Train Depot looking east

Florence was a major center in 1903, but Globe was also a rich mining community. Many of the early users of the Phoenix and Eastern Railroad were on their way to Globe from Phoenix. From newspaper articles, it seems the traveler would ride the train from Phoenix to Kelvin in one day and stay at a hotel overnight. The next day, the stage would take the traveler from Kelvin on to Globe.

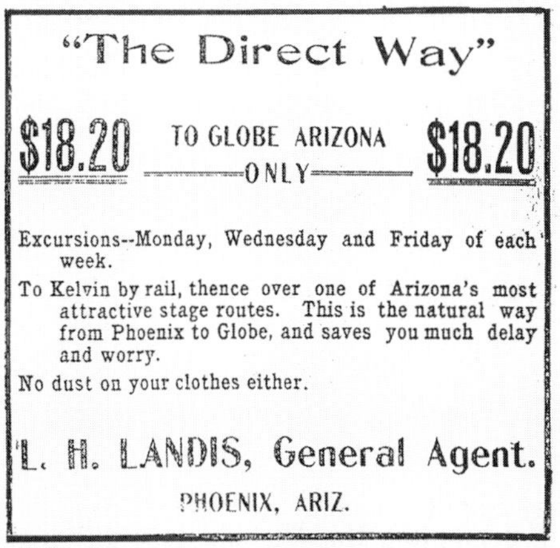
"The Direct Way"

$18.20 TO GLOBE ARIZONA ONLY $18.20

Excursions--Monday, Wednesday and Friday of each week.

To Kelvin by rail, thence over one of Arizona's most attractive stage routes. This is the natural way from Phoenix to Globe, and saves you much delay and worry.

No dust on your clothes either.

L. H. LANDIS, General Agent.
PHOENIX, ARIZ.

In 1904, the Arizona Republican ran this railroad advertisement. It is hard to imagine that you didn't get dust on your clothes on any stagecoach.

Bill Anderson began using the new railroad in 1906 to visit his sweetheart, Margaret Nelson, in Winkleman. He would catch the line at the Gilbert Depot, returning later from Winkleman. They were married in the Adams Hotel in Phoenix, Arizona in 1909. In later years, Bill and Margaret shipped many head of cattle from the Gilbert stockyard alongside the loading track.

Mr. and Mrs. T. J. Fincher and their infant son, Bruce, came to Gilbert in 1908. The train brought all of their household goods to the Gilbert depot. Mr. Fincher said all that then existed of Gilbert was the depot. All around it were alfalfa fields in every direction you looked.

As the farming grew in Gilbert, businesses began to be established. Cattle and sheep were shipped from the railroad corral. Passengers and cargo were also using the line by 1904, before the depot was built. In 1907, the Murphy venture sold out to the Southern Pacific Railroad. Even though the Southern Pacific owned the railroad, for many years it was called the Arizona Eastern Railroad.

Passengers at depot

Waiting at depot for train

The early businesses were grocery stores, blacksmith shops, a tin shop, a creamery, and the Bank of Gilbert. As a young boy I remember visiting with Robert Gamble, who told me about how busy the depot had been. Mr. Gamble married Emily Brass of one of the pioneer families in 1925. He said there was incredible traffic by hay haulers bringing their alfalfa hay to be shipped in the boxcars, which were loaded on the spur track east and west of the depot. He said some of the people would load small wagons as high as twenty feet and tie it down so they could bring it into town and ship it from Gilbert. I believe he was referring back to 1917 and through the 1920s, but even in the 1940s and 1950s there was a lot of hay shipped from Gilbert.

It was during World War I (1917–18) that the war effort was greatly assisted by Gilbert farmers and their hay shipments. In those days we still had a cavalry using horses and mules that had to be fed. Gilbert acquired the title "Hay Shipping Capital of the World" during this period of time. My 1944 fourth-grade geography book referred to Gilbert by that title. There was also a picture of trucks hauling hay to be loaded in boxcars by our depot.

Loading hay. Alfalfa hay was the major shipment from Gilbert.

In the early years of Gilbert, Main Street looked pretty bleak. Main Street is, of course, Gilbert Road, as it was initially called after the railroad spur of the same name. We have this picture that depicts those days.

Main Street, Gilbert, Arizona

OLD GILBERT HOME

The picture above is of an early home showing that each house had to drill a well to supply the water necessary for the family and for farm animals they were raising.

The home to the right was the residence of James Pine. It was built of brick and was one of the finer homes built in the Gilbert area.

Most of the early businesses were of a very simple design as you can see in the picture below of the Gilbert Bank. In 1918 when the building was constructed, Gilbert did not have a paved Main Street.

JAMES PINE HOME

GILBERT BANK: STILL STANDING AT THE SOUTHEAST CORNER OF MAIN AND PAGE.

These two pictures are of the John Anderson home. The winter photo allows us to see the simplicity of the home with its surrounding porch. A covering of plants kept the house cooler in the summer. It was probably the first "air-conditioned" home in Gilbert.

JOHN ANDERSON HOME IN WINTER MONTHS

JOHN ANDERSON HOME IN SUMMER MONTHS

Here are two more pictures of the Gilbert Depot, the hub of business in the town during its formative years.

OLD VIEW OF GILBERT DEPOT

MORE MODERN VIEW OF TRAIN DEPOT

The Creed Store was an early establishment in Gilbert.

Another early business in Gilbert was Forrest Clare's Sheet Metal Shop as shown in the picture below. Many of Forrest Clare's grandchildren and great-grandchildren still reside in Gilbert. The sheet metal shop that stood for more than eighty years is no longer on Main Street, but the old home he raised his family in still stands.

Inside the Creed Store

Forrest Clare's Sheet Metal Shop

Nowell's store was also one of the pioneer businesses in our community.

Clive Davis built one of the earliest grocery stores on the east side of Main Street. Descendants of the Nowell and Davis families still reside in the Valley of the Sun, and pictures of their families are on display at the Gilbert Historical Museum.

NOWELL'S STORE IN 1917

CLIVE DAVIS STORE IN 1918

The Barber Building was the first business built south of the railroad tracks. It was constructed on the west side of Gilbert Road just south of the railroad. It was originally a barbershop but later served as the home of the *Gilbert Enterprise*, a local weekly newspaper. This building is no longer standing, but to the rear of where the old building was there is now a fire station. When the fire station was built, it was considered a modern improvement to the station that was within the old Town Hall across the street.

BARBER BUILDING

CHAPTER III

Farming

Homesteaders began farming in the Gilbert area as soon as they could dig a small ditch from their land back to a canal in the Mesa area. Mesa began tapping into the water of the Salt River in 1877, when the Lehi pioneers settled along the Salt River. They dug out the old Indian canals, laterals, and ditches used hundreds of years before.

Jack Swilling started the first canal company in Phoenix in 1865. He was the first white man to open the old Hohokam waterways to bring water to the early farms. Even before Swilling's venture, farmers were cultivating the alfalfa that grew naturally around the Salt River bottom in Phoenix.

The first water brought to a Gilbert farm came by way of a ditch four-and-a-half miles long. It was dug from Mesa to the John Anderson farm on the east side of present day Gilbert Road, and Mr. Anderson had obtained permission to hook onto the other farmer's ditch. This was about 1892, as it took a great deal of time and effort to clear the desert of brush and cactus and prepare the land for farming.

Doctor Chandler and his associates dug the Consolidated Canal from Mesa through the Gilbert area. About 1893, they took water to what is now Chandler, Arizona. Dr. Chandler is credited with consolidating and improving the canals to make them more efficient. Prior to

Man with team using a Fresno land scraper.

some of his innovations, a lot of water was lost that the valley needed for farming.

The following map shows the early homestead entries between Baseline Road and Warner Road and between Cooper Road and Lindsey Road.

There were many other homesteads, but this area surrounds the area that would become old downtown Gilbert. The railroad dissects Gilbert Road, which became the center of town.

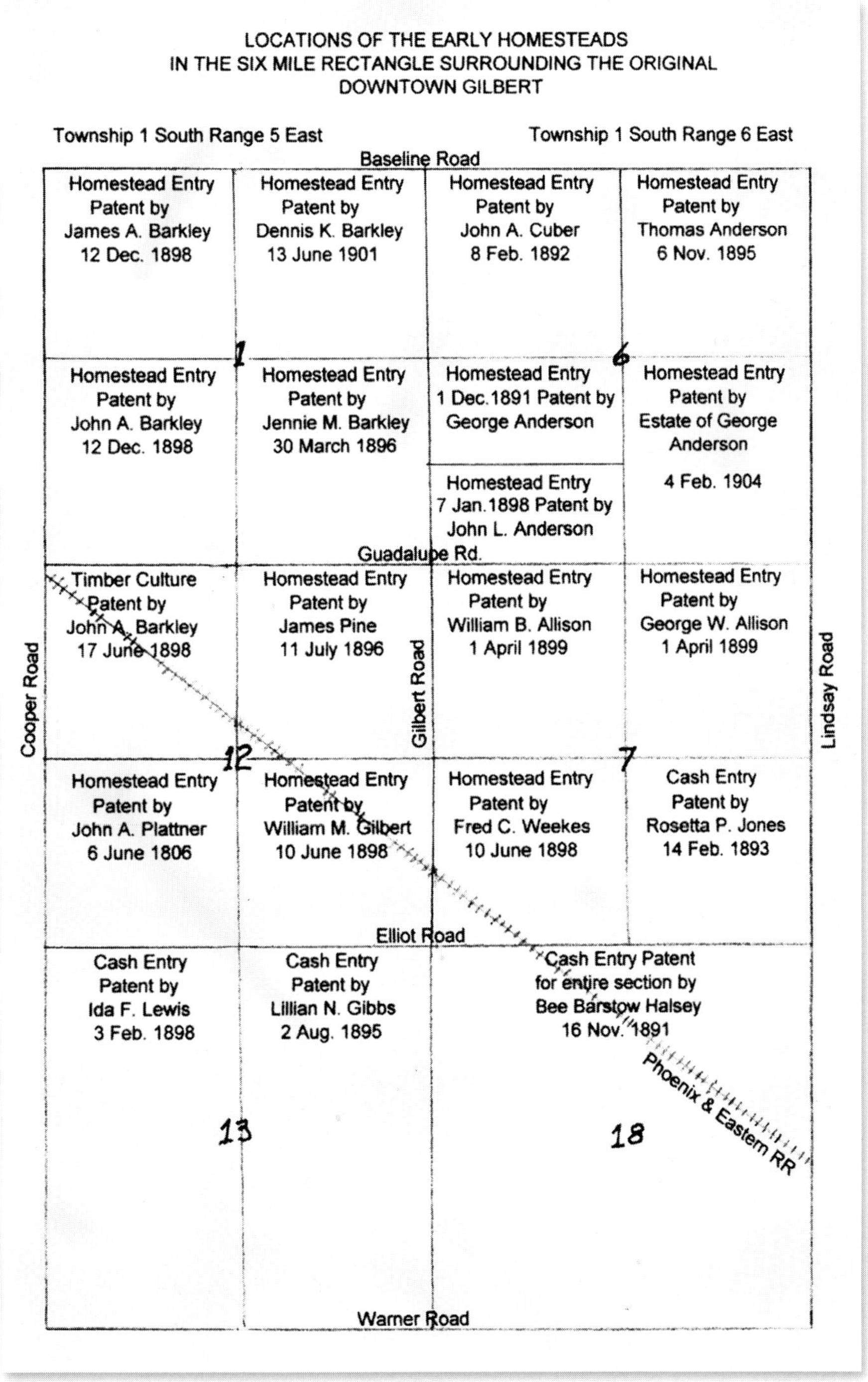

The early farmers in the area first had to clear their lands of the natural desert, level the land, find a water source, plant, and pray. They were rugged people who settled here, and the equipment they used seems foreign in our day. The Gilbert Historical Museum has many pictures in its collection of these people working their land, mainly with horses or mules as a power source.

Alfalfa hay was the major crop of our early pioneers, and the picture at right shows a hay rake that was common more than a hundred years ago.

HAY RAKE

BILL MORRISON AND TEAM

Hay baling

These are prize bulls that were owned by Amos Burk. In 1912 he brought his Brown Swiss cattle to Gilbert from Rippey, Iowa. He and his wife, Cora, built a fine home at the corner of Elliot and Gilbert Roads.

Prize Brown Swiss bulls

During the building of the Roosevelt Dam, many from the Gilbert area assisted the construction, knowing that the dam would guarantee security for farmers and their future. Bill Anderson drove freight over Fish Creek Hill to the dam site. Here is a picture of freight being hauled to Roosevelt Dam.

FREIGHT TO ROOSEVELT DAM

These are more pictures of horse-drawn equipment and hay baling, which was our most important industry in the beginning of the twentieth century. The hay sling was used by many farmers in Arizona. You can still see old ones in Utah, Idaho, and Montana. In the early 1900s, everyone in the Gilbert area was not only familiar with them but most had worked on such equipment as they handled alfalfa hay.

HAY SLING

HAY BALING IN 1920

Laboring in the fields required lots of men and animals in order to complete the farm work that had to be done to provide for pioneer families. The mule was a major asset to farmers because of its incredible brute strength.

ONE MULE

MEN AT WORK

MCFREDERICK, AN EARLY RESIDENT, WITH TEAM

These hardworking Gilbert farmers in the Arizona desert take time out for a picture. How wonderful for us to be able to see their clothing and, above all, the industry they each were willing to give for their family's livelihood.

❧ Hardworking men and beasts

❧ Just another day in the sun

❧ Industrious farmers

In the early 1900s, horses and mules were the main ingredient for work in the fields, and even mechanized equipment was assisted by horsepower. Manpower was also labor-intensive, as you see in this picture. A large group of men was necessary to operate most machinery in the beginning of the twentieth century.

Laborers pose for the camera

Juan Olgin is shown at right letting young John Olgin and Dionescio Sepulveda admire his huge load of baled cotton before delivering it to the buyer.

For more than two hundred years, cotton picking was done by human hands. Picking cotton in Gilbert was no different. It was very hard work, and the bolls that held the cotton caused lots of pain, pricking the fingers that pulled the cotton out.

HAULING BALES OF COTTON

COTTON PICKING

COTTON GIN

The cotton was processed in gins in and around Gilbert. When I was a young man, we had three cotton gins in town. This gin shown above is still standing along the tracks west of Gilbert Road.

Albert "Ab" Nichols and his oldest son, Artie, are shown below in about 1920, taking loads of baled alfalfa hay to the Southern Pacific Railroad Depot in the Town of Gilbert.

HAULING HAY TO THE GILBERT DEPOT

Fieldwork was the usual occupation of our early settlers, and everyone took their turn at what had to be done. Those were the days of hard work from sunup until sundown. Chores had to be done, and it didn't matter if you were a girl or a boy—you took your turn and saw that all the labor was done each day.

The picture on the opposite page shows a typical farm. Note the water tank that was so necessary for survival in the desert. Every home had its own well to provide water for humans and animals. Irrigation water for the fields came later by ditch and lateral, as canals snaked their way through the Gilbert area.

A threshing machine that was operating in 1919 was a modern convenience that sped up the processing of wheat for the local farmers.

Fieldwork

Early transportation

Typical farm

Threshing machine

During the early farming period, the ostrich business flourished as well. Our next-door neighbor, Chandler, celebrates its ostrich-growing era each year, but many in Gilbert may not know that we had farmers growing the big birds, too. Ostriches were grown for their plumage and their eggs as well as for meat. Some of the following pictures of ostrich farming in Gilbert are on file at the Gilbert Historical Museum.

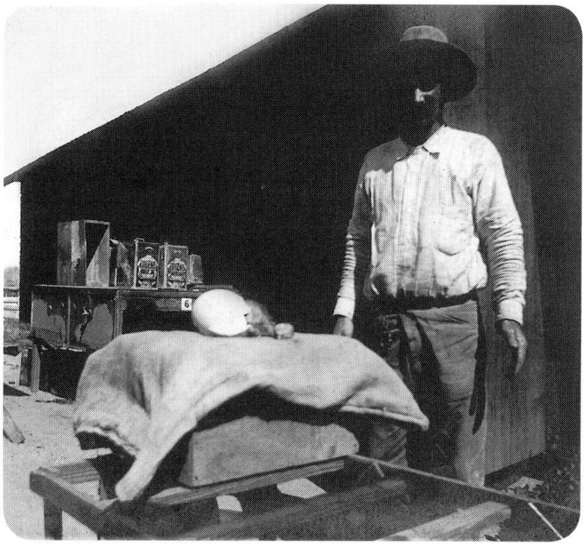

Ostrich hatchery at Baseline and Gilbert Roads

Ostrich

Ostrich and eggs

Ostrich talk

After so many years of using horse-pulled equipment to run a farm, we began to use automation. By the 1920s, there were trucks on the road hauling huge loads of cotton, hay, wheat, watermelons, cantaloupes, and other produce. The modern-day tractor was becoming more common, allowing more work to be accomplished on farms. In the Gilbert Historical Museum are many pictures of early farm machinery, as well as some of the original equipment.

Cranking car in front of farmhouse

Farmhouse

Loaded

Specialty equipment was manufactured for many uses. One of the most important aids in building ditches and canals was a trencher. The photograph shown here depicts the trencher with both a caterpillar crawling system and the round wheels that were used more often. America was in a period of building any usable item that could be designed by man. The economic boom of America was driven by our great manufacturing technology and our need to expand farm production to supply America and the world with our produce.

Close-Up of Trenching machine

Trenching machine

EARLY TRACTOR

In the early 1900s, many entrepreneurs who created better systems and equipment came out of the industrialization period of America. Farmers in Arizona as well as all over our great country were taking advantage of the new innovations. In this great push to modernize, tractors and harvesting equipment were becoming better and better.

ANOTHER EARLY TRACTOR

MODERN TRACTOR EVOLVING

After great success in alfalfa hay production, Gilbert became a major producer of cotton. Both short-staple and long-staple cotton were easy to grow with a sure supply of water. The dams that were built in the watershed areas made the growth of farming and the Town of Gilbert a natural phenomenon.

Trucking farm produce

More trucks in Gilbert

Cattle were raised in the fields in Gilbert as well as on the desert east of town. Many of these cattle were shipped from the corrals alongside the railroad just east of the Gilbert Depot. Cattle were driven down Guadalupe or Elliot Road from east of town right to the corrals for shipment. Farms were being established with all the amenities of the Midwest. Below is a picture showing the replacement of cactus and sagebrush with trees around homes in the Gilbert area.

After President Theodore Roosevelt enacted the Bureau of Reclamation Act, he directed the building of the dam. Construction began at the confluence of the Salt River and Tonto Creek in 1904. To even begin the enormous project, roads had to be dragged to the site so equipment could be delivered as needed. The work went on for seven years. On March 18, 1911, President Roosevelt dedicated the dam bearing his name.

FARMHOUSE WITH TREES

ROOSEVELT DAM 1961

Making all the farm growth possible were the large canals passing through the Gilbert farm area. The Consolidated Canal that was built by Dr. Chandler and his associates to take water to the Chandler area was a boon to all the farmers along its path. Later there was the Highland Canal to the east of the Consolidated, but the Eastern Canal later replaced that. We generally referred to the Consolidated as the First Canal and the Eastern as the Second Canal. Both these canals fell under the management of the Salt River Project, which has maintained all the irrigation from the Second Canal west across most of the Salt River Valley. The Third Canal was established by the Roosevelt Water Conservation District and is headquartered in Higley, a subsidiary of Gilbert.

Roosevelt Dam made our valley blossom and created Roosevelt Lake. The other dams below Roosevelt are the Horse Mesa Dam that backs up Apache Lake; Mormon Flat Dam that created Canyon Lake, and Stewart Mountain Dam that gives us Saguaro Lake. There is also Granite Reef Dam, and all of these are on the Salt River. On the Verde River above Granite Reef Dam, there is the Horseshoe Dam that gives us Horseshoe Reservoir, and Bartlett Dam, which backs up the Bartlett Reservoir. These dams hold the water reserves necessary for the Salt River Valley to exist and flourish.

THE FIRST CANAL IN GILBERT 1910

This is only a small depiction of the vast irrigation system that has made farming such a miraculous success in Gilbert for more than one hundred years. Not only has our farming community brought us alfalfa hay, cotton, watermelons, cantaloupes, lettuce, tomatoes, potatoes, corn, wheat, maize, pecans, onions, carrots, and pistachio nuts, but countless other food products as well.

As a community, we are thankful for farmers putting our town on the map. We are now taking vast amounts of our farmland and developing massive residential housing and commercial developments in what used to be open fields. Gilbert is moving toward becoming a mega-residential community.

A TYPICAL OLD PUMP-HOUSE ALONG A CANAL

CHAPTER IV

Schools

In 1891, a new school district was created for the south Mesa area. It was organized as District 41 of the Highland School District and was initially administered by the Mesa School District. The first frame schoolhouse south of Baseline Road was constructed in about 1900, in what would become Gilbert.

The large Barkley family that came to Arizona in 1886 gave the school district its first and second school site. These were the Barkleys who had homesteaded more than a section of land south of Baseline Road. Their first parcel was homesteaded in 1898. The first schoolhouse on this donated land was built at the corner of Cooper Road and Baseline Road.

In essays written by John Sawyer and Rose Divelbess, both longtime Gilbert residents, the school was described as follows: "A one-room lumber building with a porch on one side for protection in bad weather was erected on this corner [Baseline Road and Cooper Road]. A hitching rail was provided for students who rode a horse to school. The horses were tied to the rail and they waited patiently until school was dismissed. Sometimes a small amount of hay was brought along on which the horse could nibble."

We know from family history records on file at the Gilbert Historical Museum that Morris Cooper attended school in this one-room schoolhouse in 1907. He was one of the children of the large Orson Cooper family for whom Cooper Road is named. Mr. Cooper also served as mayor of Gilbert from 1959 to 1967.

First school in Gilbert (pencil sketch drawn by Leilani Wilson)

HIGHLAND SCHOOL—GILBERT'S SECOND SCHOOL

This first school served the area until 1909, when a better schoolhouse was built one mile south on another parcel of land donated by the Barkley family. This two-room, cement-block building was constructed before school began in 1909. It was called Highland School because it was built on one of the highest elevations in the area. It is interesting to know that Hubert Sawyer and his family had moved to Arizona the same year from Indiana. Mr. Sawyer helped in the building of the school and then taught classes there for the next two years.

In 1912, the area was growing so fast that the school board decided to build another school at the corner of Elliot and Gilbert Roads, on five acres given by Everett R. Wilbur and his wife Nelly. Everett's father, who was a doctor, had given the quarter-section of land to the young couple when they married. Everett was very talented as a dairyman, blacksmith, and machinist, and was also an inventor. When Gilbert was incorporated in 1920, he became Gilbert's first mayor.

The first Gilbert Post Office was established in 1912 at the same time the school board was approving the new schoolhouse. The board also decided to change the school district name to Gilbert School District Number 41. The building, constructed in 1913, consisted of four classrooms, a central assembly room, two small offices, and a large entryway into the building. There was also a large basement in the west center section of the original building. This building had no inside plumbing, but there were two outside toilets and a well south of the building that furnished fresh water. A furnace in the basement under the assembly room provided heat in the winter.

In 1916, a bond election approved ten thousand dollars to build a north wing to the elementary school. This consisted of two basement rooms and two classrooms just above ground level. By the time this section was built, a water fountain was supplied for teachers and students.

Gilbert's Third School, now used as the Gilbert Historical Museum

First Gilbert High School

Among the students in the first grade in 1916 were two young girls who rode their horses to the new elementary school at Elliot and Gilbert Roads. One was my mother-in-law, Velma Anderson, whose grandfather was the first to develop homestead entry land into a farm. His name was John Anderson, and his son farmed that property until his death in 1946. The other horseback rider to the Gilbert school was Marian Bond. She later married Alfred Pine, the grandson of James Pine, another Gilbert pioneer. Photos of the two ladies and their first-grade friends are on display in the School Room at the Gilbert Historical Society.

This building was an elementary school only, but by 1915, area residents were asking for high school classes to be offered as well. Prior to that time, all students went to Mesa to receive a high school education before Gilbert had a high school. After 1915, some of the elementary school teachers taught high school courses in their spare time.

The old Gilbert High School was completed in 1920. The building cost $125,000. It was a two-story building with classrooms on both floors and a very large auditorium. By 1920, grades seven through twelve were taught in this new building.

In the early 1920s, an evaporative cooler fountain was built in the back of the elementary school. When I started school in 1941, that large fountain with eight outlets was still there and was a most welcome convenience.

THE SCHOOL DISTRICT AS IT APPEARED IN 1945

In 1925, the school board approved $10,641.60 to build a south wing on the old elementary school in order to provide two more classrooms. It was 1927 before bathrooms were added to the west end of the north and south buildings. In the 1940s, the boys' bathroom was on the south and the girls' bathroom was on the north side.

The Brookins family moved to the Gilbert area from the Black Hills of South Dakota in 1909. Their daughter Gertrude was eleven years old. In the records of the Gilbert Historical Society we find that she rode her pony to the block school in 1913 when she was the lone graduate from the eighth grade. Gertrude Brookins was one of the first four graduates from Gilbert High School.

An interesting aspect of the Gilbert High School is that some students graduated from the high school before the high school building was built. This happened because of dedicated grammar school teachers who tutored high school classes to those who wanted a high school education. Four students graduated with Gilbert High School diplomas in 1918. The graduates were Myrtle Lines, Elvin Lines, Linda Marsh, and, as previously mentioned, Gertrude Brookins.

In 1918 and 1919, high school senior classes were graduated in ceremonies held on a platform extending from the west entrance to the north wing of the elementary school.

School busing was not established in District 41 until the 1925–26 school year. Prior to that time, students provided their own transportation to and from the school.

On the previous page is an aerial photograph of the school district as it appeared in 1945. The road in the foreground is Gilbert Road, and in the top right we can see Elliot running east toward its intersection with Gilbert Road.

Beginning from the right side of the picture is the Gilbert Elementary School, which was built in three phases in 1913, 1917, and 1927. The next building in the middle of the picture is the Gilbert High School that was built in 1920. To the left of the high school is the old gymnasium and to the left of it is the Mexican School. Behind the gymnasium is the manual arts building and behind that is the bus barn. To the right rear of the high school building is the outdoor combination tennis and basketball courts.

GILBERT ELEMENTARY SCHOOL IN 1945

GILBERT MEXICAN SCHOOL

SCHOOL FOR BLACK STUDENTS

From the 1920s until 1951, Gilbert had a segregated school for Mexican children in grammar school. Above is a photo of the building they attended. The building is now used for accounting offices for the entire Gilbert School District.

In the 1920s, this home in Gilbert (right) was used to teach the few black students who lived in Gilbert. The house was near the water tower but has been torn down.

In 1940, a small two-room building was built to the west of the south wing of the elementary school, providing two first-grade rooms. Mrs. Tissaw taught in the larger east-side room, and Miss Applebee taught my class on the west end in 1941.

Even though the old Gilbert Elementary School continued to be used until the 1970s, new brick cottages were built for classrooms to the west and south of the old school building. These units were built in 1954 and have been used continually as they are today in 2007.

The original high school that was built in 1920 became the Administration Building when a new high school was built in 1965. That building is now Mesquite Junior High School. The current Gilbert High School was built in 1985 on the south side of Elliot Road east of Lindsay Road.

In 1980, the entire elementary school complex was rented and later sold to the Gilbert Historical Society in 1982. The Historical Society has been able to maintain the building with the wood floors and the same basic classrooms now serving as a museum to educate people about the wonderful history of Gilbert from its meager beginnings in the early 1900s. This museum building was placed on the National Register of Historic Places in 1980.

From 1975 until today, the Gilbert School District Number 41 has continued to expand. It is building new schools to provide for the needs of the community, which has grown from the original handful of pioneers to today's 190,000 inhabitants. Our schools have had to keep up. We currently have twenty-six elementary schools, six junior high schools, and six high schools. A proposed high school and an elementary school are currently on the drawing board.

CHAPTER V

"Gilbert"

William M. "Bobby" Gilbert (1859–1945) was twenty-three when he came to Gilbert in 1882 from Missouri and settled in the Mesa area. Bobby and his father were very active in buying and selling real estate in the east valley.

Many have asked why William M. Gilbert went through his life known as Bobby Gilbert. Having been born in Missouri in 1859, he grew up admiring General Robert E. Lee and chose to be called Bobby in honor of the great general. It is interesting, however, that he signed all his official land transactions with his birth name of W. M. Gilbert.

In 1882, land in the east valley was selling for $1.25 an acre. Bobby immediately began his life of land speculation. It was because of the opportunity to acquire land economically that he filed and received his homestead entry patent June 10, 1898, on the Southeast quarter of Section 12, Township 1 South, Range 5 East of the Gila and Salt River Base and Meridian. This parcel of land is currently bounded by Gilbert Road to the east, the Western canal to the north, the half-section line to the west, and by Elliot Road to the south.

Four years after Bobby Gilbert became the owner of his 160 acres, a railroad investor named Frank Murphy came to see him. Murphy wanted a right-of-way for his railroad through his quarter-section. The land lay in the pathway to the mineral deposits to the east. Gold and copper had been found along the Gila River in the Winkleman and Kelvin area of Arizona. Murphy wanted his railroad to be a part of the development of the mining industry. Murphy and Gilbert came to two agreements. One of the contracts was for the main line and the other for the spur line and depot.

Frank Murphy had to acquire the rights-of-way along his entire planned route to Winkleman. He attempted to get landowners to donate the rights-of-way to enhance the value of their property, but he also paid those who wouldn't donate them. In Murphy's negotiations with Gilbert, he did pay one hundred dollars or more for the first mainline deed, which was sixty-six feet wide. The second parcel was for sixty-seven feet in width.

The Phoenix and Eastern Railroad's first right-of-way purchase from Bobby Gilbert was dated October 24, 1902. The second strip, for a spur line and the site for an eventual depot, was deeded on December 14, 1902.

The actual construction of the railroad brought the train through Gilbert in 1903, when there were very few homes in the area. They belonged to those who had acquired homesteads to raise cattle and eventually to farm. This was prior to the Consolidated Canal coming through the area.

On the second track right-of-way, the following was agreed to: "all necessary spurs, side tracks and structures usually appurtenant thereto, within the limits of a strip of land sixty-seven feet in width being parallel with the existing right-of-way." It was this siding that would first carry the name "Gilbert" when we were still part of the Arizona Territory.

Not long after the track was laid in 1903, shipments of cattle from the new Gilbert Siding were being loaded and shipped to Phoenix and other points east. We have records of cattle shipments in 1904 from Gilbert. The Gilbert depot was not built until 1905 after the Phoenix and Eastern was better established.

The spur track that was built was called Gilbert. The section line road that ran north and south through this area became known as Gilbert Road. Gilbert was established as a name in history even before there was a town beside it.

In 1903, there were only a few pioneers living in the area. These families were the forerunners of all the future farmers that came into the area after adequate irrigation water was available. Following these early inhabitants came merchants that took root on Gilbert Road near the Gilbert siding.

William M. "Bobby" Gilbert (1859–1945)

John Sawyer and Rose Geiszl Divelbess assisted each other in sketching Gilbert in 1918, as they remembered it from their youth.

The oldest building in the drawing below is the Gilbert Depot, which was constructed in 1905. The Ayers-Butler Grocery was built in 1910, and Houck's blacksmith shop was established in 1912. The Nowells' home was built about 1915. Gilbert's first pharmacy was built in 1916 and called Pilchers Drugstore. In 1916, Timmons Garage was built, and in 1918 it became the Tone and Blakely Garage. North of the garage is Clare's 1917 sheet metal shop. The Gilbert Bank was also built in 1917.

Spindler's Grocery and Meat Market was our second store. In 1918, Clive Davis came to town and built the third store, calling it a General Store. J. D. Lynch built the first lumberyard in 1918. Burns built the second blacksmith shop, and Mr. Barber built the Barber Building, the first store south of the railroad tracks.

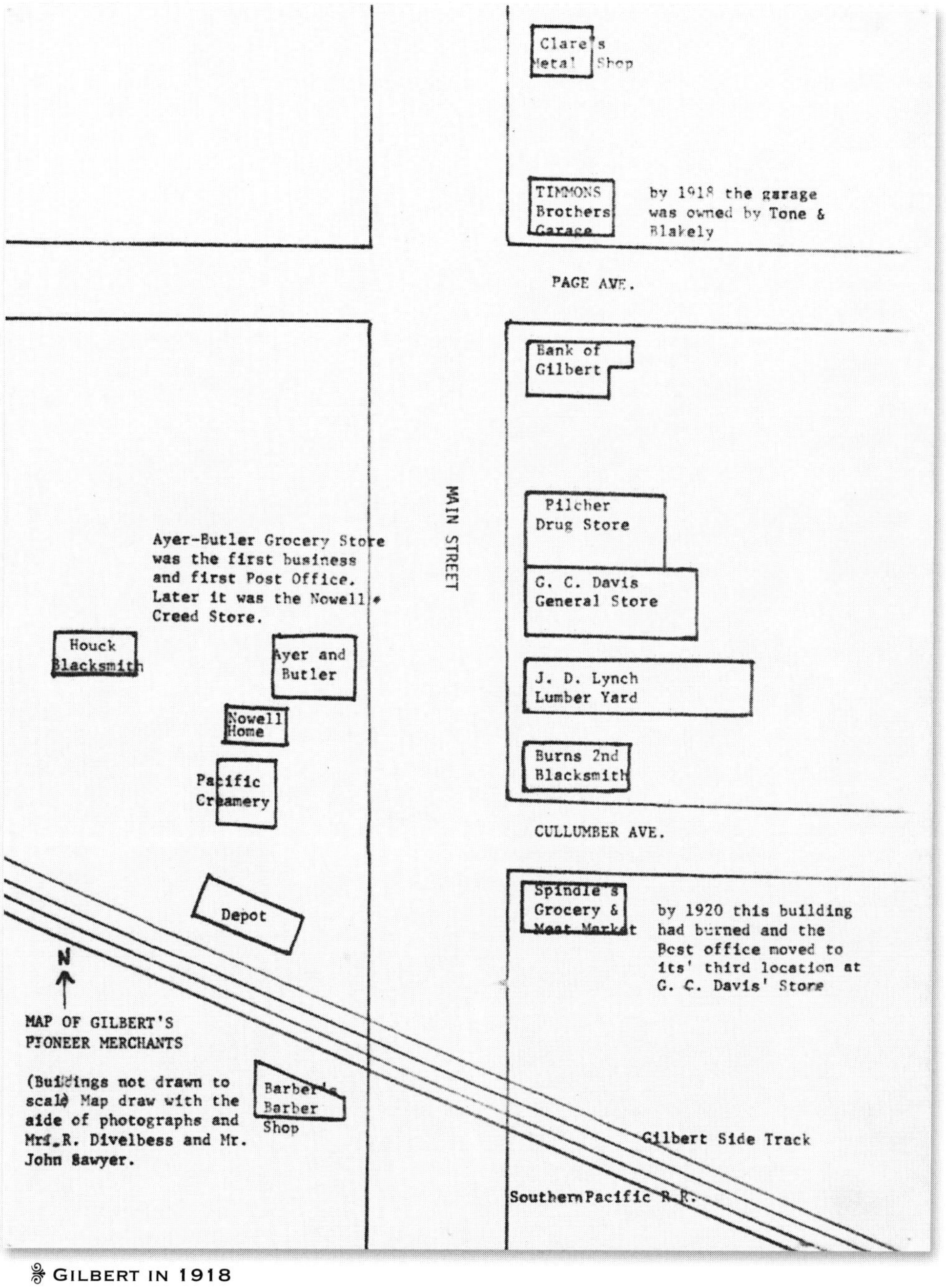

GILBERT IN 1918

In 1914, a subdivision known as the Gilbert Townsite was recorded in Maricopa County. We now think of this area as "Old Town." This filing was two years after Arizona was granted statehood and six years before Gilbert became an incorporated community. Gilbert became an official town in 1920 when the incorporation was filed under the laws of the State of Arizona.

At right is the original Gilbert Townsite plat, which was filed on April 13, 1914. This document reads in part: "that E. S. Welch, A. W. Ayers and Cora E. Burk, administratrix for the estate of Amos Burk, deceased, have this 21st day of April 1914 subdivided under the name of Gilbert townsite. The subdivision was approved by the County of Maricopa, State of Arizona."

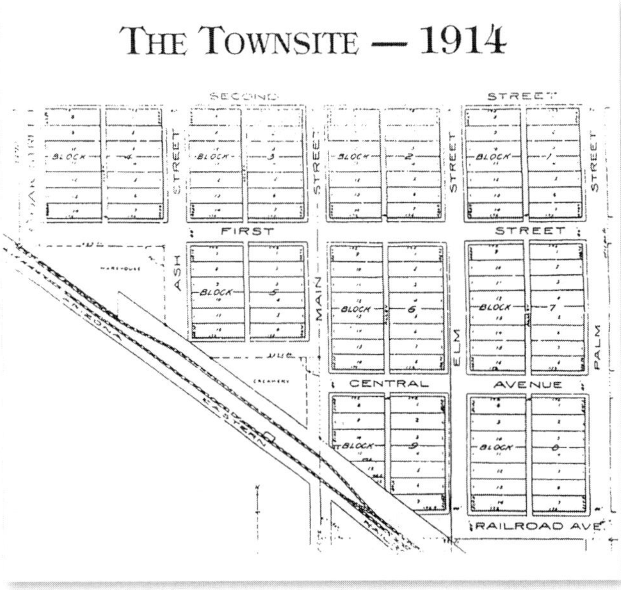

GILBERT TOWNSITE

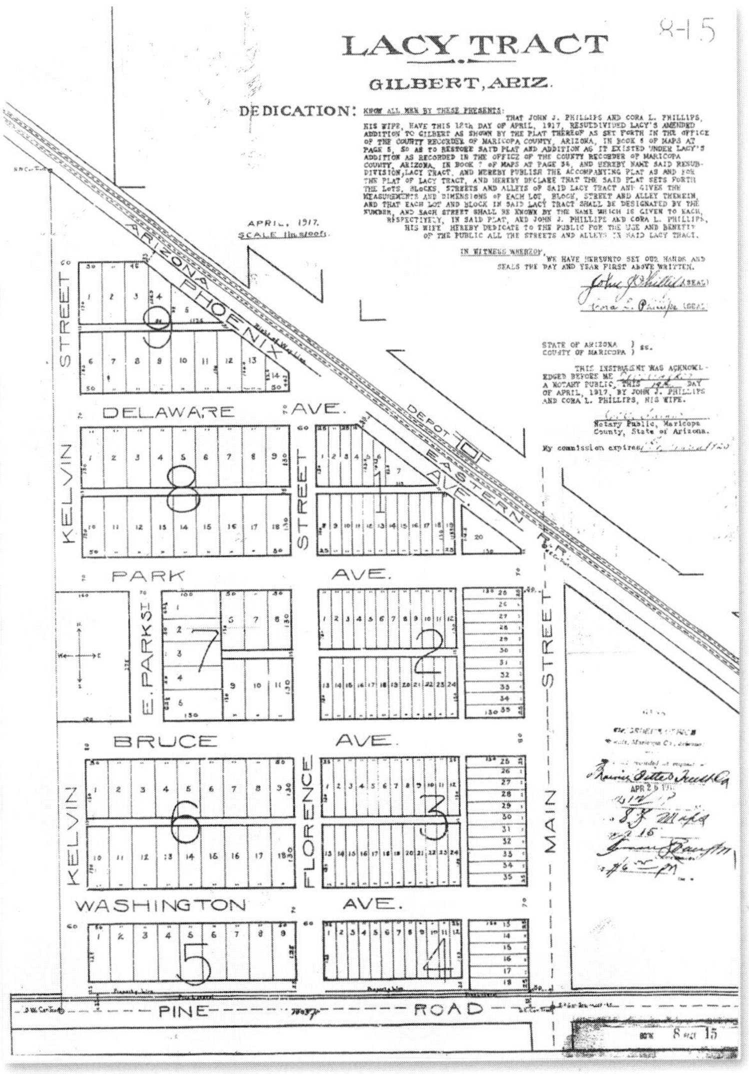

LACY TRACT, 1917

In 1917, the second subdivision was recorded in the future Gilbert. It was called Lacy Tract (left) and was filed by John J. Phillips and Cora L. Phillips, his wife, on the twelfth day of April, 1917. Phillips recorded an amendment on April 19, 1917 changing East Park Street to Oak Street.

The events of history often cause the naming of roads and communities. In our case, Gilbert was named for the location. The railroad was going through the area, and the land just happened to be owned by Mr. Gilbert. A community is what it becomes because of the good people that inhabit the area. The pioneers of our community shared their talents, guiding our town into good works by developing education, roads, water systems, sewer systems, electrical systems, phone systems, and all the other blessings of modern life. All of these things were not in place when Bobby Gilbert homesteaded his land. Bobby Gilbert is the father of our town, even though I am sure he had no idea what would come of the siding track called Gilbert. The events of history have created Gilbert. It is exciting to know that the name "Gilbert" has been attached to our community for over a century now.

The following pictures are of other homes and buildings that existed prior to Gilbert's incorporation. The home below was typical of homes in 1911, as it had a large porch where the residents and friends could visit without being in the direct beams of the sun. The business on the right was in downtown Gilbert in 1915. You can see the Eating and Drinking sign on the right side of the picture. We don't know if the "drinking" was beer, hard liquor, iced tea, water, or milk.

Front porch scene at a home in Gilbert in 1911. The bed on the porch shows how people slept outside to stay cool in the summer.

Dixie Club in 1915: "Eating and Drinking"

During the period of time prior to Gilbert's incorporation there was a financial depression, America was involved in World War I, and an influenza epidemic killed many United States citizens. A number of those who died in Gilbert are mentioned in the family histories of our early settlers. Representing men from Gilbert who served our country during World War I is Jake Sanborn, shown below.

Jake Sanborn, serving in the First World War

Three Gilbert men were part of this Mesa National Guard Unit.

In addition to a war going on in Europe, Gilbert was doing the usual things that small farming towns were doing in the era of the 1920s. Some of the town leaders in those days are shown here. On the left is Mick Johnson, who came to Gilbert in 1919 and built "Mickey's Café," which he ran for many years; to his right is Leland Barber, who built the Barber Building about 1917, which had a restaurant in it; to his right is Dr. Lucius M. Tompkins, Gilbert's first doctor who came to Gilbert in 1919; and on his right is Leslie Creed, who came in 1912 with his merchant family.

MICK JOHNSON, LELAND BARBER, DR. LUCIUS M. TOMPKINS, AND LESLIE CREED

HOME FROM A SUCCESSFUL DEER HUNT: CLEVE WEST, FRANK RAMSEY, ED MCCREARY, MORRIS COOPER, AND BOB MERRILL

❧ Gathering of a few Gilbert ladies

❧ High school basketball team, 1918

The ladies of Gilbert also knew how to have fun in the 1920s. Here are a few in their modern swimsuits, taking the time to be photographed for the viewers of the future.

Our ancestors were hard workers, but they also knew how to have a good time and enjoy spare time and holidays.

In addition to the other activities, Gilbert also had its own basketball team that had very interesting exercise clothing. They wore knee pads to protect them from floor scrapes. As you see, they were a handsome lot.

Picnics were a wonderful way for townspeople to get together, to gather and socialize as a community.

❧ Truck loaded with fun-loving people

A GRAND PICNIC, ABOUT 1918

1918 VIEW OF GILBERT ROAD

Gilbert Road was dirt in 1918. The space between the photographer and Gilbert Road is where the first Town Hall was later built. In the right corner of the picture is the Barber Building that was built in 1911. The home is the original Harmon home. To the far left is the Gilbert Elementary School, which was built in 1913 with the north wing added in 1917. The cameraman was standing on the rise of the railroad track foundation.

Charles Blakely took over Timmons Garage in 1920, and his sons followed his example and built Blakely stations all over Arizona.

GILBERT GARAGE

Dublin and Page was one of the new, modern stores of the 1920s. This building is still standing, but it now houses modern furniture. Gilbert still had dirt streets in 1920, which are visible in the picture. There were concrete walkways in front of the stores, however. Almost all stores had overhangs for protection from the sun.

❧ DUBLIN AND PAGE: "DRY GOODS, SHOES, GROCERIES"

Mr. Cosby came to Gilbert in 1917 to go into business. He chose the real estate profession. He was a fancy dresser and must have been an impressive, self-assured gentleman. Abe Cosby also sold insurance, and his office on Gilbert's Main Street was where he made many plans for the improvement of his adopted town. In addition to his real estate business, Abe also was instrumental in the creation of the Bank of Gilbert and served on the bank board.

Abe Cosby Land

Abe Cosby, Real Estate

The Bank of Gilbert

Even before Gilbert became an official community, it already had three major churches established with their own buildings. The Church of Christ was the first church to build its own facility in 1914, followed in 1918 by the Mormon Church. The First Methodist Church was built in 1919. The Catholic residents attended church in Mesa prior to building Saint Anne's Catholic Church.

CHURCH OF CHRIST, BUILT IN 1914

L.D.S (MORMON) MEETING HOUSE, BUILT IN 1918

FIRST METHODIST CHURCH, BUILT IN 1919

SAINT ANNE'S CATHOLIC CHURCH, BUILT IN 1934

In the 1920 census, Gilbert was already a diverse area, with 584 Mexican settlers and 996 Anglo inhabitants. It needs to be understood this was the count in the trade area of Gilbert. The town population was much smaller than the total of 1,580 people in the census count. This count did not include the Higley area, as their numbers were recorded separately.

The incorporation of the Town of Gilbert took place on July 6, 1920, and the first Mayor of Gilbert was Everett Wilbur, shown below in his dress best. It appears from our best research that there were only five hundred souls in the town proper at the time of incorporation. The initial town land in the Town of Gilbert in 1920 was approximately 814 acres.

EVERETT WILBUR, GILBERT'S FIRST MAYOR

One of the things the new town council wanted to accomplish was the development of a consistent public water supply. Their ambitious plan was to build a water tower that would supply a gravity flow system to the citizens of Gilbert.

In 1925, the Gilbert Town Council contracted to build the water tower. In the early years of the water tower, it was painted black, but from the 1930s until early 2007 the tower was painted silver. It is now white. The dreams of the town were fulfilled upon the completion of the water tower and the pipe system created in 1925.

The water tower is shown below as it is in the middle of town and only one block west of Main Street (Gilbert Road).

GILBERT WATER TOWER PAINTED BLACK

MODERN GILBERT WATER TOWER

A pump-house was built below the tower and was used many times as the first jailhouse in Gilbert. On Sunday mornings, it was fun to walk by the jail and hear the drunks from Saturday night moaning in our little adobe jailhouse.

FIRST JAILHOUSE

CHAPTER VI

Depression and War

On October 29, 1929, the American stock market collapsed. America entered a period we now call the Great Depression. Every person in America as well as the world was affected by the decline of the United States dollar. Middle America was hit especially hard, because many farmers relied on balloon payment notes with their local banks. When the banks went under, foreclosures on farms became rampant. In addition to the bank failure was the ecological phenomenon known as the Dust Bowl. Farmers and laborers became destitute and began looking for survival wherever they could find it. Arizona began receiving people from three major states—Arkansas, Oklahoma, and Texas. The influx of these migrants into Gilbert created a real change.

The Dust Bowl was the worst recorded natural disaster in America. The topsoil was blown off the land in severe dust storms. Without water and land cover, these states were devastated. Families sold their meager assets and began to travel west. Most were on the way to California, but Arizona absorbed a great many who offered cheap labor wherever they settled. Gilbert's population in 1930 was 791, but by 1940 it was reported to be 837. These numbers don't reflect the growth in the farm area as most of these new settlers lived on the farm owner's property where they worked.

A tent camp was built by poor people south of Gilbert on the east side of the road before getting to Warner. They called the area "Okie Camp" because most of the new arrivals were from Oklahoma. They picked cotton, worked on combines and hay balers, dug ditches, irrigated, and did any odd job that provided a few dollars to feed their families. At this same time there was a large tent camp at Val Vista and Main in Mesa. That camp was called "Oklahoma City." The residents eventually found work and homes, and both of these camps had disappeared by 1940.

The influx of these workers helped to start greater farm production and services in the Gilbert area. Most merchants allowed credit to people in the area because most were only paid every two weeks and some were only paid once a month. Times were hard for everyone, and the people of Gilbert worked through this period as did other communities all over America.

The outcome of this low economic period was to make people very frugal and more appreciative of basic things such as housing, food, and good health. This toughening of the people is reflected in the history of Gilbert. Below is a picture of Main Street looking south. It must have been a Saturday as there are so many cars on the street. In the 1930s and 1940s the vehicle parking was angle parking rather than parallel. This picture is my favorite view of old Gilbert. I remember it like this from my childhood. The Gilbert sign and the Gilbert water tower meant "Welcome Home."

MAIN STREET LOOKING SOUTH

Main Street is paved, looking north from railroad track

The aerial picture shown here is of Gilbert in the mid-1930s and gives a very clear view of Gilbert and its minimal progress from the scenes of the 1920s. There was a lot of vacant land, as it was a typical small town in the depression years.

This picture has been used to build a Gilbert Diorama which is on display in the Town Room of the Gilbert Historical Museum. There was little change in the town from the time of this picture and the mid-1940s other than a few newer cars.

The aerial picture on the following page gives a good view of the Railroad Depot, which was the hub of business from its beginning in 1903 through the 1950s. The Barber Building in the bottom center of the picture became the home of the Gilbert Enterprise in 1929, which served as our weekly newspaper for many years. The water tower is visible on the west side of Main Street. On the right side of Main Street in the middle of the picture is the red brick building that was built in 1929 for the Pay-n-Take-it store. It was built where the old Timmons Garage and later the Tone and Blakely Garage had been. We remember the building as the Tone Building because the Tones built it. The super grocery store did not last, due to the Great Depression. The large building on the west side of Main Street is the Blakely Building.

THE BLAKELY BUILDING

TOWN OF GILBERT LOOKING NORTHWEST

BLAKELY MOTOR CO.
WALTER W. PAGE
GILBERT, ARIZ.-No.2

GILBERT'S MAIN STREET, LOOKING NORTH

THE BARBER BUILDING

THE TONE BUILDING

In addition to the great financial dilemmas of the 1930s, Gilbert was flooded in 1931 and again in 1938 (photos, pp.79-81). It was generally accepted that the heavy rains that fell in those two years dropped so much moisture that the canals and the land could not absorb the rainwater. That was certainly true, but there was another theory proposed about the 1938 flood. East of the Gilbert farm area in the desert, the land was so saturated that the water just began rising and topped out at three feet or so above ground level. All this water naturally flowed west as the elevation decreases in this direction. As the water headed west, it ran into the base of the railroad track, which directed the water northwesterly right into downtown Gilbert. In the 1930s, Gilbert didn't have flood control.

The flood can't stop Otto Neely from delivering the milk.

Crossing street during flood

Gilbert Lake?

Water, water everywhere

Blakely Motor Company moved up from the smaller garage to a deluxe building on the west side of Main Street. Even with the floods they were able to continue to manage their operations, including a restaurant that Mrs. Luella Blakely managed in the northeast end of the complex. Luella called the restaurant the El Nopal Café.

BLAKELY'S AND SERRANO'S

BLAKELY MOTOR COMPANY

The Gilbert Depot was an interesting point, because the other side of the tracks did not have any water. The railroad track acted as a dam. The flooding of the basement of Sam Lee's Grocery Store caused the wrappers to come off the cans, and for the next year they sold cans of food that were a surprise to the person who opened them.

GILBERT DEPOT DURING THE FLOOD

SAM LEE GROCERY STORE

WADING ON MAIN STREET

CAN'T DRIVE THROUGH THIS!

DON'T ENTER WHEN FLOODED.

WOMEN'S CLUB FLOODED TOO

WOMEN ENJOYING THE FLOOD

IF WE MUST WADE, WE MUST.

In 1935, the Works Progress Administration (WPA) was created by presidential order to give employment, build needed highways, bridges, and buildings, and provide other services to help bring America out of the Great Depression. In 1938, the Gilbert Town Hall was approved as one of the association's projects, and the WPA constructed the building, which is shown below. This is the site of the current Chamber of Commerce.

GILBERT TOWN HALL

After the Timmons/Blakely Garage was torn down, the Tones built this super grocery store for the Pay-n-Take-It chain. The store was built in 1929, and the bank failure caused the demise of this new business, too. Joe's Bar-B-Que is here now.

THE TONE BUILDING

One of the new businesses in the 1930s was the Capital Fuel, Feed, and Seed Company. Capital provided feed and seed for the farming community. It also purchased alfalfa and other products grown by the farmers.

The Capital Company was located just north of the Gilbert Depot, where products and produce were received and shipped. This north exposure of the depot displays the best view of the beautiful Spanish-style structure.

Northern exposure of Gilbert Depot

Capital Fuel, Feed, and Seed Company

CENTRAL MARKET AND LIBERTY MARKET

SERRANO'S AND MICKEY'S CAFÉ

Frank Erramuzpe came to Gilbert in the 1930s and married Flora Locarnini, a local girl. The Locarninis had established their home in Gilbert in 1913. Erramuzpe was a sheep farmer who raised his sheep in Gilbert in the wintertime. He herded his sheep north to the Mogollon Rim area in the summer for grazing in the cool country. The Gilbert stockyard shown at right is thought of as an outlet for cattle grown in the area, but it was also used by sheep farmers.

ERRAMUZPE AND HELPERS LOAD SHEEP AT THE GILBERT STOCKYARD

Gilbert and America were still struggling through the Great Depression on September 1, 1939, when Germany invaded Poland as a prelude to World War II. In the early years it didn't appear that the United States would be involved in another European war, but the war continued to expand. Eventually we came to the support of our allies by sending them food and other supplies. As the German submarines began sinking our supply ships, we became more and more involved in the Great War.

Japan also wanted to be a world colonial power, and as early as 1931 they attacked Manchuria and later China in 1937. We called Germany and Japan the Axis Powers after World War II broke out.

On January 7, 1941, our military headquarters in Hawaii was attacked by Japan, an ally of Germany. This led to America's declaration of war against Japan on December 8, 1941. Germany declared war on America on December 11, and in return we declared war on Germany on the same day. Everything in Gilbert changed, and many of our local men and at least one woman joined the Army, Navy, and Marines. In 1941, we didn't have a military department called the Air Force, but we had the Army Air Corp. The United States Air Force was not formally created until September 18, 1947.

During World War II, the United States was forced to ration many products. Gas, rubber, and sugar were rationed to American families. Ration stamps for these products were distributed to those who needed them. We were also encouraged to grow vegetables in our own Victory Gardens.

In March of 1941, the United States Congress passed the Lend-Lease Act to provide aid to our Allied Forces. A great shortage of meat existed in England, and the Hormel Company began shipping millions of tins of processed meat to them. It is said that Spam was not as good in 1941 as now, but those who had very little meat or none at all desired any form of beef or pork.

After millions of people died during World War II, it finally came to an end. Germany surrendered on May 2, 1945, and Japan surrendered on August 14, 1945. Gilbert and our farm area had many volunteers that went to war to stop the aggression of these two imperialist nations.

On the following pages are some pictures of those who served our country during World War II. We as a community salute them for their heroic service to keep America free. The people who served are honored in the Military Room of the Gilbert Historical Museum. There is a War Memorial Monument dedicated to those valiant people in front of the museum, too. This brief exposure helps us to remember how our citizens responded to the need of our nation.

Real Admiral Raymond Weldon Burk was born in Gilbert, Arizona, on December 31, 1920. After graduation from high school in 1938, he enlisted in the United States Navy. After boot camp in San Diego, California, he served as a Seaman on the U.S.S. Arizona. While there he was given the opportunity to attend the Naval Academy Preparatory School. After passing the entrance exam, he became a Midshipman at the U.S. Naval Academy in Annapolis, Maryland. He graduated from the academy in June 1943. Burk then served aboard destroyers and an aircraft carrier. He retired in July 1976.

Rear Admiral Raymond Weldon Burk

The four Gieszl brothers all enlisted in the military service after the breakout of war. William Joseph, Carl Raymond, Hugh Lynn, and George Scott Gieszl all became officers in the branches they served in.

William Joseph Gieszl

Carl Raymond Gieszl

Hugh Lynn Gieszl

George Scott Gieszl

The four Lemons brothers also enlisted into the military service. Eugene E. Lemons served in the United States Army from 1941 to 1945. Clarence E. Lemons served in the Army, too. Lois G. Lemons served in the Marines and younger brother Ray R. Lemons served in the Navy.

COXSWAIN RAY R. LEMONS

STAFF SERGEANT CLARENCE E. LEMONS

SERGEANT LOIS G. LEMONS

CORPORAL EUGENE E. LEMONS

From the Everett Wilbur family, the first Mayor of Gilbert, there were three members of the family who served. Ethel Wilbur Mastin was a Storekeeper Second Class in the U.S. Navy Waves. Joseph H. Wilbur was a Corporal in the Army Air Corps. Walter F. Wilbur was a Lieutenant Colonel in the Army Air Corps.

Second Class Storekeeper Ethel Wilbur Mastin

Lieutenant Colonel Walter F. Wilbur

Corporal Joseph H. Wilbur

During World War II, Glen Martin, a local barber, began collecting pictures of young men serving in the armed services. In 1991, a collage of those pictures was attached to a three-by-four-foot backing by Geraldine and Albert Nichols and placed in the Gilbert Historical Museum. It now hangs in the Military Room and displays seventy or more Gilbert veterans of World War II. Some of those pictures are shown in the next few pages.

KENT TONE

DANNY ISCH

REGGIE BEEBE

BILL BISHOP

A. J. HUNTER

IRVIN AND EVERT PEDEN

LEVI AND WALTER PAYNE

MEREDITH MILLER, JR.

ROSENDO MARTIN

BOB ANGLE

J. T. HUNTER

HEROLD COLLUMBER

EUGENE NEEDHAM

JACK MONTGOMERY

FRANK ESTRADA

Albert Nichols

Bill Johnson

Earl Nichols

Rowdy Hughes

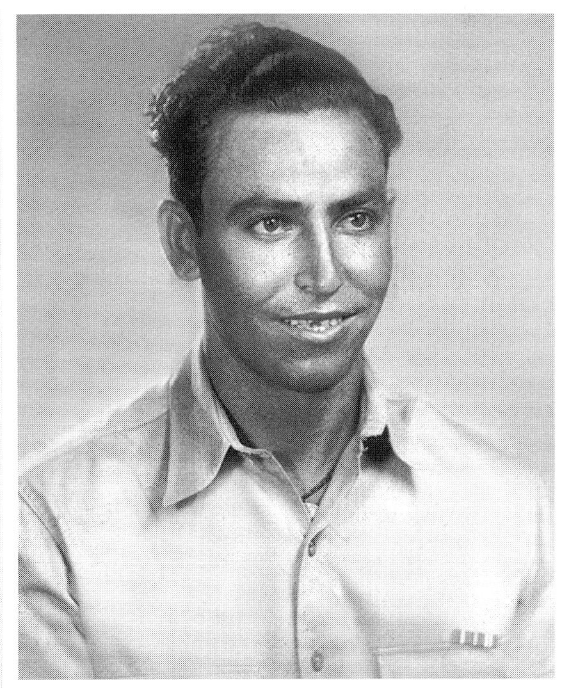

Edward Virzuela

ARTIE L. NICHOLS

LARRY HUFFINES

ALFRED SOTOMAYOR

LAWRENCE NEEDHAM

DON CLARE

PERCY HUFFINES

BILL WALLACE

ROBERT BOLEN

GRANT NEAGLE

LEE MCKINNEY

TILL ROSALES

CORTEZ BOHANNON

LUTHER C. NASH

GAYNOR CONNOR

EDMUND VERRUE

EUGENE CARRISOZA

JOHNIE E. BURUATO

Carlos Padilla

Marvin Morrison

Kenneth Morrison

Lloyd Nash

Mike Sotomayor

George Bernard Drain

The photographs inside Sam Lee's Grocery Store would be typical during the war years. Note the signs hanging above the family that ran the store. The vegetables and fruit are displayed in large wooden boxes.

SAM LEE GROCERY AND THE FAMILY

INSIDE VIEW OF SAM LEE'S STORE AND THE FAMILY

For years Hap Nowell's Pharmacy was a hub of activity, not only for medicine but the daily update on local news. Farmers and others from the community met there to catch up on the latest events.

HAP NOWELL IN THE PHARMACY

OLD-STYLE PHARMACY

INSIDE BLAKELY'S SECOND HAND STORE. GEORGE HARMON, THE MANAGER, IS IN THE MIDDLE.

In 1945, as our young men and women came home from the war, the Gilbert Airport was conceived and built. Joseph H. Wilbur and Bill Mastin, his brother-in-law, started the Wilbur Flying Service. Bill Mastin had learned to fly in 1939 and had become both an expert airplane mechanic and a certified pilot and flight-training instructor. Bill and Joseph decided to teach others to fly. They built the airport on Wilbur's land and began flying their small aircraft over the east valley. Many people in Gilbert came to see them fly and to go sightseeing. Some of them signed up to learn to fly.

One of their students was Darrell Sawyer, who later created Sawyer Aviation in Phoenix. Darrell was in high school when he began flight training. John Goodman was a pilot during the war and came to Gilbert to be a science teacher. He took me for my first flight from the Gilbert Airport in 1949, when I was fourteen. We flew from the airport and over the east valley. It was spectacular to have such a broad view of the farm area below and was a very exciting opportunity. I never picked up the bug to learn to fly myself, but many did. Bill Mastin taught several hundred Gilbert residents to fly during the years the airport was open.

The airport and lounge and the airport and hangar are shown below. They were the headquarters for the Gilbert Airport. Classes were conducted in the lounge, and many local men like Albert Serrano, Dick Miller, Dave Lamoreaux, and Willie Rosales were taught to fly and received their own flight certifications here.

GILBERT AIRPORT

Shown left is an aerial view of the hanger and the runway next to it.

After the airport was abandoned, the hangar became Spec Conner's cabinet shop for the new housing boom that began in the 1970s. Today, the swimming pool and park area next to Mesquite Junior High sit on the airport landing strip.

GILBERT AIRPORT FROM THE SKY

GILBERT AIRPORT FROM THE GROUND

Pilots and planes that were flown from the Gilbert Airport are shown below.

DICK MILLER

RAY SEYMOUR

BILL MASTIN, TEACHER

DARRELL SAWYER, STUDENT

In a recap of Gilbert police protection, it should be said that in the early years we had a Town Marshall to protect us. Our first Town Marshall was Oscar Phelps, who served the community beginning in 1920. In 1930, Marshall George Harmon was Town Marshall, and in 1950 his brother, Hubert Harmon, served in that capacity. Fred Dees was hired in 1975 as the last Town Marshall, and in 1977, Marshall Dees became the first Chief of Police in Gilbert, Arizona.

You can read more about our police officers, Marshalls, and Gilbert's chiefs of police in D. L. Turner's book *From Star to Shield*. She has created a very informative book.

Chief of Police Fred Dees

Town Marshall Oscar Phelps

Town Marshall George Harmon

Town Marshall Hubert Harmon

Gilbert's fire protection was afforded to our citizens by a volunteer organization for many years. The town council purchased fire protection equipment including trucks and fire engines. In recent years, Gilbert has created a professional emergency services organization that is as modern as any in America. Below, however, let us look at our old fire-fighting equipment and a couple of the volunteer teams that served our community.

1960s FIRE-FIGHTING VOLUNTEERS

1950s FIRE-FIGHTING VOLUNTEERS

TOWN HALL AND GILBERT FIRE DEPARTMENT

CHAPTER VII

Infrastructure—1950s through 1980s

The sewer system was installed throughout Gilbert beginning in 1947. Developers began to look at the Gilbert area as a place to build homes on cheap farmland. One of the first modern subdivisions was Gilbert Estates, built by Irvin Peden in the mid-1950s. Irvin grew up in Gilbert and continued development the remainder of his life. The Gilbert Estates subdivision is west of Gilbert Road and south of Elliot. The streets are a quarter-mile long and the homes are less than a thousand square feet—up to 1,230 square feet on average. The lots are also small, but much larger than the original lots in Gilbert that were only twenty-five feet wide and one hundred feet deep. The homes are on Catalina Street and Sahuaro Street. Our 1,230-square-foot home on Catalina Street was purchased for $11,300 in 1959. Below is a picture of the home initially built for Dr. Bill Statler in 1954 on Sahuaro Street. The home typifies the size and style of that era.

Most homes in Gilbert were frame construction from the 1920s and '30s and were built on the narrow twenty-five-foot wide lots. A frame home on Delaware Street across from the Southern Pacific Railroad Section houses was sold to my dad in 1939 for two hundred dollars. The home consisted of two rooms, which my dad soon expanded to three bedrooms, a small living room, and a kitchen. There was no indoor bathroom, but there was an outside privy. People bathed in large washtubs in those days, and children all had a bath on Saturday morning. Later, a cesspool was dug and an inside bathroom was installed, making the home very modern for the 1940s. It was after the sewer system was built that people hooked their disposal systems to the new service.

1954 HOME IN GILBERT ESTATES

❧ 1920s HOME, STILL SERVING EIGHTY YEARS LATER

Above is a picture of one of the old homes that sits on Gilbert Road. It has been decorated for the current business in the house, but the dimensions have not changed from the 1920s when it was originally constructed.

For over sixty years, this home (right) has been occupied by one of the Sagasta family. The left side of the home was added to the original dwelling. For those of you that do not recognize the structure on the roof, it is a swamp-cooler used before modern refrigeration.

❧ ANOTHER HOME FROM THE 1920s

Tom Clement, Mayor of Gilbert from 1947 to 1953, came to Gilbert in 1934. He is now ninety-five years old. During his mayoral reign, the council agreed to put a sewer system into the town. It was a major infrastructure necessary for the community to become a modern city.

In 1953, merchants Albert Serrano, Dan Valenzuela, and others decided to add some interest in Gilbert by creating a Cinco de Mayo Celebration. In the first years, it amounted to having a dance on Main Street but soon became a parade and a dance. The townspeople loved to come and see all their friends at these parties each year. This festival was the beginning of the Gilbert Days Celebration that is now held on the third weekend in November.

During the term of Mayor Kenyon Udall in 1956, all the streets in the town limits were paved. Prior to 1956, the only paved streets were Gilbert Road (Main Street), Elliot Road, and the two new streets in Gilbert Estates. These were laid in 1953 in conjunction with the new subdivision.

The Gilbert Days Celebration fit perfectly after the streets were paved, and different volunteers aided the organization of the parade entrants. The tradition has continued for more than fifty years and is a highlight of the Town of Gilbert.

Geneva Clay organized the early years of the Gilbert Days Parade. She served the community as a councilwoman, in the Gilbert Chamber of Commerce, and as a volunteer for a multitude of projects. Bob and Judy Lowry later managed the parade and Gilbert Days. Bob was also a councilman and Judy was President of the Gilbert Historical Society. We owe them all a great debt of gratitude.

Thousands of people have participated in the Gilbert Days Parade.

GILBERT DAYS PARADE

Downtown route

Horse in parade

Old Glory celebrated in 1976 parade: Two hundred years of freedom

Youth make the Parade.

In 1971, a new law was enacted that increased the town council to seven members from five. The old procedure for seventy years had been that the councilman who received the most votes would become the mayor. The seven new members elected me, Dale Hallock, as mayor. I had served as the Planning and Zoning Commission Chairman for the previous year.

As an escrow officer in the title insurance business, I invited many builders to come to Gilbert and build homes. Jalma Hunsinger came to Gilbert and began building Hunsinger Homes. Jalma later built a subdivision called College Park Country Estates on Guadalupe Road. The house-per-acre idea brought many to the area to enjoy the farm climate available in the 1970s and '80s.

Among many builders who came to the area during this time were the Brimhall brothers, who built the Rawhide Subdivision. Building continued, bringing many people to town during the 1970s and setting the stage for further growth.

In 1972, the Town Council hired Lynn Stuart as the first Town Manager and began to modernize the town. Prior to this time, the clerk of the town ran things.

In 1974, Lynn Stuart and I worried that Gilbert was going to be run over by Mesa to the north of us and by Chandler to the south. We decided to encircle our town with a strip annexation to stop the manifest destiny by those two communities. The strip annexation required landowners, mainly farmers, to sign an annexation petition agreeing to our annexing them into Gilbert. Ordinance No. 174 was presented and approved on January 8, 1975. A copy of the annexation map attached to the ordinance is shown below.

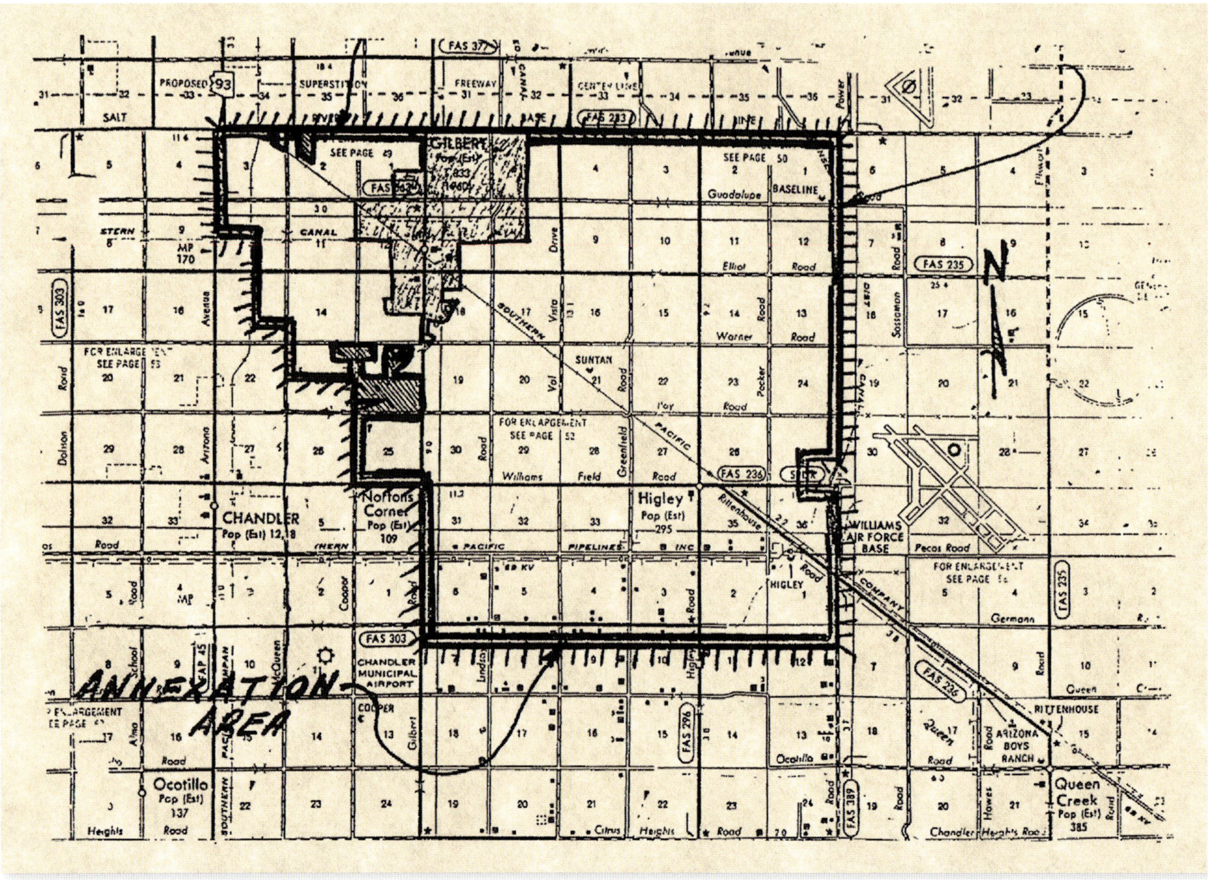

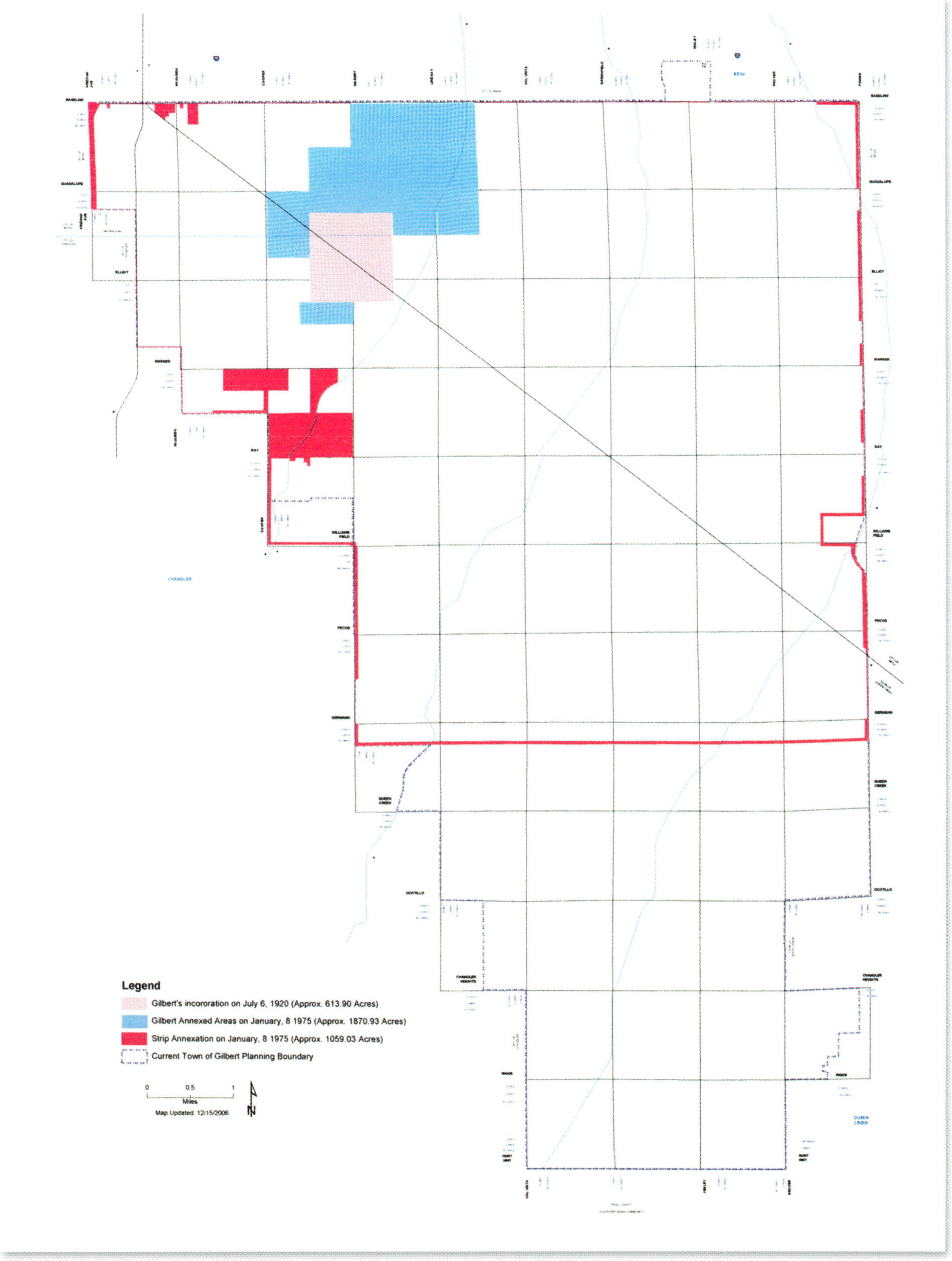

GILBERT AND THE 1975 STRIP ANNEXATION

The light pink area was Gilbert in 1920, and the blue area was annexed on January 8, 1975, along with the outer striped line and other parcels that are shown in red.

In 1965, the Gilbert Chamber of Commerce recommended that all the stores in Gilbert change their storefronts to a Western style. Most of the merchants in downtown Gilbert went along with the idea, and the town designed sidewalk overhangs to look Western.

GILBERT TOWN HALL WITH WESTERN MOTIF

TOWN HALL AS MODERNIZED IN 1982

In the 1970s, the idea of selling one or two acres with house and horse privileges became very popular in Gilbert. Many people living in the east valley came to Gilbert to have their own personal farm on one or two acres.

RANCHO LAGANTE ON ELLIOT ROAD

HORSES IN COLLEGE PARK COUNTRY ESTATES

Circle G Ranches developed many of the house-per-acre subdivisions throughout the Gilbert area. At right is one of their typical entrance signs.

White Fence Farms Company also developed house-per-acre subdivisions.

CIRCLE G RANCHES

WHITE FENCE FARMS

As we move on to the residential growth of Gilbert, remember that for decades the land mainly grew alfalfa and cotton. The growth has been greatly enhanced because of Route 60, the freeway from Phoenix to the east valley. Interestingly, in 1975 the Gilbert Town Council predicted that Gilbert would contain eighty thousand people by 2020. The freeway heading east toward Mesa and Gilbert was not given a lot of consideration with regard to how it would impact new growth. The general plan was that in addition to the Town of Gilbert, there would be a trade area around Higley and perhaps Norton's Corner. Norton's Corner was located at the northwest corner of Williams Field Road and Gilbert Road. It was a major watering hole for the drinking man and woman.

Below is a last look at a growing cotton field, a farm product that is now being replaced by the growth of homes.

COTTON FIELD

CHAPTER VIII

New Growth

The Gilbert Historical Society has been preserving artifacts since the late 1960s. Before that, there were many who cared for the histories, memories, and belongings of the early pioneer families. In 1973, there was a resolution by the Gilbert Town Council acknowledging the Gilbert Historical Society and their desire to preserve the past. This pictorial history has been gleaned from the Gilbert Museum archives and from individuals who had personal pictures and histories not yet on file.

The Gilbert Historical Society was fortunate to rent the old Gilbert Elementary School building in 1980, where they began displaying the town's artifacts. A great deal of renovation was necessary to make the building a public museum. The efforts of those early society members are not only acknowledged but also greatly appreciated. In 1982, the Gilbert School Board agreed to sell the building and the present site of the museum to the Gilbert Historical Society. Otto and Edna Neely donated three hundred thousand dollars for the purchase and the expense necessary to make a museum of the building. They and other contributors are honored in the halls of the Gilbert Historical Museum today. A picture of the museum is shown below. As you wish to become more familiar with the history of Gilbert, the Gilbert Historical Society invites you to come and browse, to reflect, and to appreciate our pioneers.

Now we will look at current history being made by the growth of our community.

GILBERT HISTORICAL MUSEUM IN 2006

A major breakthrough in modern resort living was created by the development of Val Vista Lakes at Baseline Road and Val Vista Drive. From the beginning of Val Vista Lakes, people have recognized Gilbert as an up-and-coming housing area for the Valley of the Sun. This progressive master-planned community included lakes of water throughout, creating a resort oasis in what had been a sleepy farming community.

Beautiful landscaped hills and waterfalls at Val Vista Lakes

Entrance to Val Vista Lakes

Since its opening, the beautiful Val Vista Lakes Clubhouse has been used for club meetings, banquets, wedding receptions, and many major Gilbert events. It is an outstanding facility that measures up to the finest country clubs in the valley.

Val Vista Lakes Clubhouse sign

Val Vista Lakes Clubhouse

On the west side of Gilbert at Elliot Road and McQueen, The Islands was created with lakes and gorgeous landscaping. Many have found their homes there near the manmade lakes.

The North Shore

The Islands of Gilbert

The Groves of Gilbert were created within old Doc Rowell's (Dr. Frank D. Rowell) pecan grove. The existing trees enhanced the homes. The Groves are located on East Elliot Road, adjacent to the Consolidated Canal.

THE GROVES OF GILBERT

RIDGEWOOD, ANOTHER OF GILBERT'S SUBDIVISIONS

Another of the many new subdivisions that have small lakes within the development is Wind Drift, located along Elliot Road east of Lindsay Road.

ENTRANCE TO WIND DRIFT

FOUNTAIN SURROUNDED BY A LAKE IN WIND DRIFT

By the close of the twentieth century, the new subdivisions were driving a population explosion in our town. Gilbert was officially the fastest-growing community in America.

MADERA PARC

The Western Skies Golf Course was the first golf course built in growing Gilbert.

WESTERN SKIES GOLF COURSE

BOYS AND GIRLS CLUB IN GILBERT

The old Mormon Church became the Boys and Girls Club of Gilbert. In 2007, the building was demolished, and new offices and shops will be built on the corner of Washington Street and Gilbert Road (Main Street.)

After years of using the old Mormon Church building, the Boys and Girls Club constructed their own facility two blocks to the east of their original site in Gilbert. Many young people benefit from the opportunities afforded them at the new Boys and Girls Club, shown left.

OLD MORMON CHURCH THAT BECAME THE BOYS AND GIRLS CLUB

For those residents who have lived here since the 1950s, downtown Gilbert is known as "Old Town." The more recent name for this area is the "Heritage District." As the community continues to grow, the Town of Gilbert has preserved the old water tower, which will be the center of Water Tower Park. The old Tone Building, which has been used for so many businesses, is now the very popular Joe's Real Bar-B-Que. The town has also widened Gilbert Road and added islands, decorating them to beautify this district.

New islands on Gilbert Road

Joe's Real Bar-B-Que

Freestone Park is one of the large parks created by the Town of Gilbert. Later, the town built Freestone Recreational Center on Guadalupe Road just west of Lindsay Road for use by the citizens of the community.

FREESTONE PARK

FREESTONE RECREATIONAL CENTER

Many Stake Buildings and Ward Buildings have replaced the old Mormon Church that was built in 1918.

On the original site of the first Saint Anne's Catholic Church, Saint Thomas Byzantine Catholic Church was built. Saint Anne's replacement buildings were built on east Elliot Road.

A NEW CHURCH OF JESUS CHRIST OF LATTER-DAY SAINTS (MORMON) STAKE CENTER

SAINT THOMAS BYZANTINE CATHOLIC CHURCH

There are many new churches in Gilbert, but the new Saint Anne's Catholic Church serves one of the largest Catholic congregations in the valley.

❧ ENTRANCE TO SAINT ANNE'S CATHOLIC CHURCH ON ELLIOT ROAD

❧ SAINT ANNE'S CATHOLIC CHURCH AS SEEN FROM NORTH PARKING LOT

Members of the Church of Christ built their first church in Gilbert in 1914, and it was replaced by the beautiful building shown below.

❧ GILBERT CHURCH OF CHRIST

GILBERT'S FIRST UNITED METHODIST CHURCH

The new complex built by the Methodist Church (above) is the third facility the congregation has built in Gilbert. The building is located on Cooper Road.

The Baptist Church has had churches in several locations in Gilbert, and the Southern Baptist congregation recently built a very large complex of buildings at the northwest corner of Elliot and Recker Roads. The Gateway Fellowship (at right) offers a home to the many members in the Gilbert area.

The New Hope Community Church (bottom) is one of the many new churches that have located in Gilbert in the past twenty years.

GATEWAY FELLOWSHIP SOUTHERN BAPTIST CHURCH

NEW HOPE COMMUNITY CHURCH

Here are three of the new high schools that have been built to keep up with the great increase in population moving to Gilbert, Arizona.

MESQUITE HIGH SCHOOL ON MCQUEEN ROAD

In 1993, the procedure for electing a mayor in Gilbert changed. On March 9, 1993, the council approved an ordinance that all future mayors will be elected directly by the citizens of Gilbert. Mayor Wilburn Brown was the first to receive his election direct from the people and began serving on July 1, 1993.

After more than fifty years in the old Town Hall, Gilbert built a modern Town Hall on Gilbert Road south of Warner Road. Below is a picture of the new facility.

HIGHLAND HIGH SCHOOL ON GUADALUPE ROAD

GILBERT HIGH SCHOOL ON ELLIOT ROAD

NEW GILBERT TOWN HALL

CHAPTER IX

Massive Growth

Gilbert continued to grow exponentially during the 1990s, and in 2007, the word "growth" is synonymous with our town. Homes, apartments, shopping centers, parks, schools, and businesses have been built on almost every section of land in Gilbert.

POLICE DEPARTMENT
(PHOTO BY MARK BENNETT)

In addition to this new building, and within the Gilbert Civic complex, is the Planning and Development Building.

NEW COURTS AND POLICE DEPARTMENT BUILDING

TRILOGY

Trilogy has become a major center for celebrating activities in Gilbert and is known for its wonderful banquet facilities.

Power Ranch is one of the large new subdivisions that are attracting many to the southeast area of Gilbert.

POWER RANCH

Crystal Point Estates is one of the water park subdivisions that have attracted many to this Gilbert location because of its ski lake.

CRYSTAL POINT ESTATES

The Spectrum development is one of the larger developments in south Gilbert.

THE SPECTRUM

With the rapid increase in population in Gilbert came a need for housing. Many apartment units were built from 1990 through 2007. Sahara Palms and Playa Palms near Arizona Avenue and Baseline Road are among those complexes.

SAHARA PALMS

Page Commons is a new development near the downtown area of Gilbert.

PAGE COMMONS

The new Santan Freeway provides fast access to employment and brings greater clientele to valley-wide businesses, creating even more growth in Gilbert.

SANTAN VILLAGE PARKWAY IN GILBERT

The Town of Gilbert has decorated the bridges and tunnels with depictions of the railroad past of our town.

UNDERPASS ON THE SANTAN VILLAGE PARKWAY (PHOTO BY MARK BENNETT)

In an earlier map provided by the Town of Gilbert, there were no curved streets in Gilbert, but with the coming of The Islands and the new Santan Freeway, there have been changes. The map below is a 2007 overview of Gilbert.

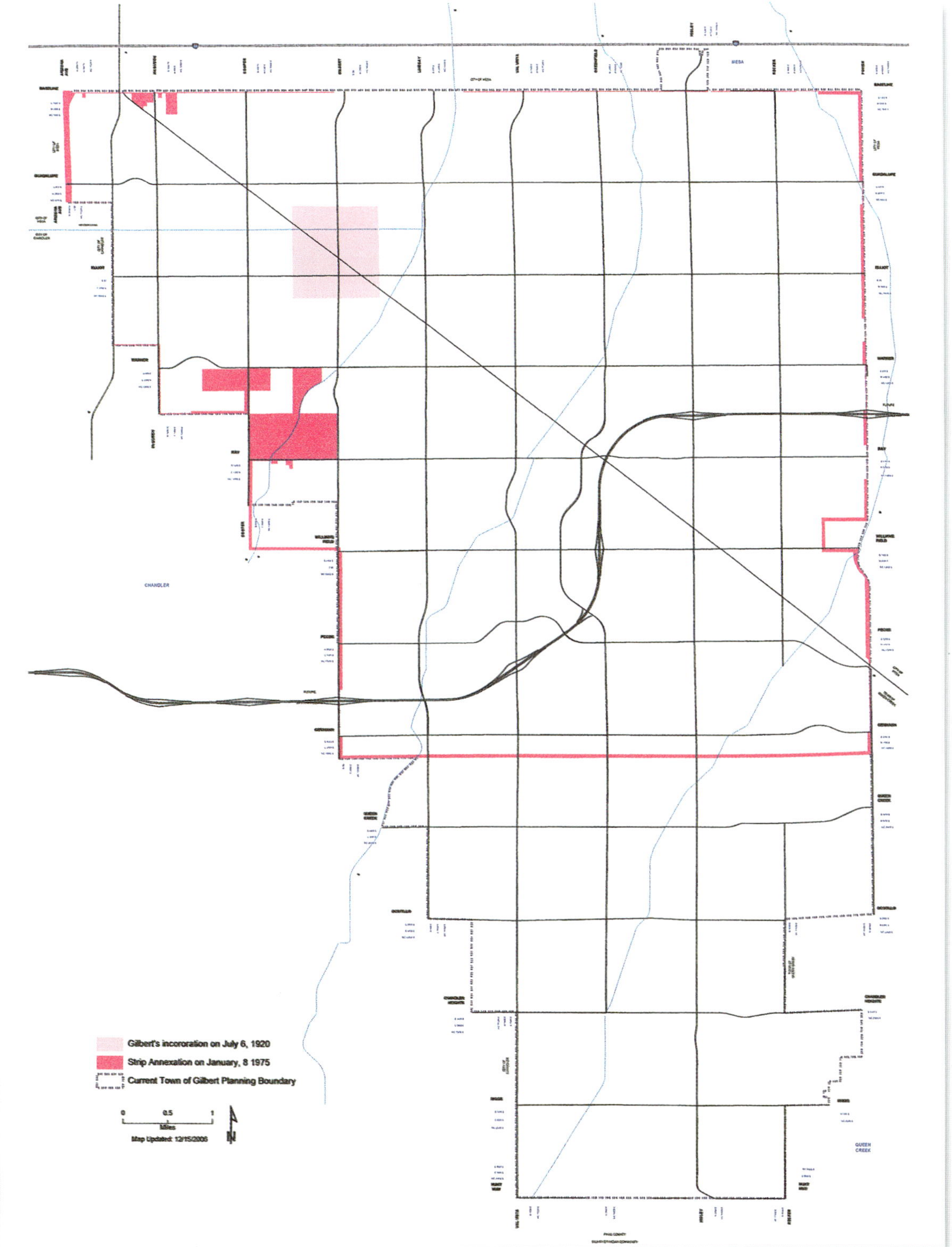

GILBERT IN 2007

The Highlands Apartments are being constructed in the Spectrum area of south Gilbert and are typical of new housing in the beginning of the twenty-first century.

HIGHLAND APARTMENTS UNDER CONSTRUCTION

ENTRANCE SIGN OF HIGHLAND APARTMENTS

Opposite: This shows San Tan Village under construction in southeast Gilbert. The sign in the foreground projects the shopping center as a completed development.

San Tan Village (Photo by Mark Bennett)

Below is a picture of some of the completed San Tan Village, with shoppers enjoying the shopping outlets.

SAN TAN VILLAGE

Following the success of the Gilbert Fine Arts Association and the enthusiasm shown by those interested in the arts, Hale Centre Theatre serves the community with wonderful entertainment.

HALE CENTRE THEATRE

Among the many beautiful parks that the Town of Gilbert is building is the new Cosmo Park, shown below. Cosmo Park is dedicated to dog owners who wish to have a grassy area where their canine friends can run. "Cosmo" was the first K-9 officer in Gilbert and has since passed away.

Cosmo Park, near the Santan Freeway (photo by Mark Bennett)

Gilbert began when cowboys and sodbusters first came here in the 1880s, and below we see two modern cowboys looking at the construction of homes as development fills our town. This growth has created the mega-residential community we still call Gilbert, Arizona. In the closing chapter, you will see our first full-service hospital. Mercy Gilbert Medical Center is a crowning achievement for the Town of Gilbert.

Riding into modernity
(photo by Mark Bennett)

CHAPTER X

Mercy Gilbert Medical Center

A History of Caring

Mercy Gilbert Medical Center is proud of its place in Gilbert history as the town's first full-service, acute-care hospital. While the hospital's history is relatively short—its doors opened on June 5, 2006—the people who brought the hospital to Gilbert have a long and rich history of caring for Arizonans. It was the Sisters of Mercy, the order of Catholic sisters who sponsor Mercy Gilbert, who in 1895 brought Arizona its first hospital—St. Joseph's Hospital and Medical Center in Phoenix. And it was Catholic Healthcare West (CHW), the system of forty-three hospitals that operates St. Joseph's and Chandler Regional Hospital, that recognized the need for healthcare services in the rapidly growing southeast Valley—especially in Gilbert, which was widely known as the fastest-growing town in America.

The Mercy Gilbert name honors the Sisters of Mercy, the hospital's sponsoring congregation. The Sisters of Mercy was founded in the early 1800s in Ireland by Sister Catherine McAuley, who had a special love for the virtue of mercy.

The Sisters' philosophy is based on the Judeo-Christian ethics of faith and love and is expressed in service, compassion, and the recognition of each person's basic human right to be treated with dignity and respect.

MERCY GILBERT MEDICAL CENTER LOOKING EAST

The Sisters of Mercy first came to the Valley in 1892 to build Sacred Heart School in Phoenix. It wasn't long before they took up another cause: to care for the tuberculosis sufferers who often died alone. The Sisters were so moved by the sick that in 1895 they opened Arizona's first hospital, St. Joseph's Hospital, now home to the renowned Barrow Neurological Institute and one of the state's leading teaching hospitals.

AERIAL VIEW OF MEDICAL CENTER UNDER CONSTRUCTION

Keeping Up with the Growth

As Chandler Regional Hospital continued to expand capacity and service offerings to meet the needs of the steadily increasing population of its neighbors to the east, it became apparent to that hospital's leadership, as well as CHW leadership, that the southeast Valley would soon face a shortage of capacity in local hospitals.

For the next two years, Chandler Regional Hospital leadership conducted feasibility studies, worked with local officials, analyzed community healthcare needs, and sought out an ideal location to build the area's next hospital. They found that perfect location, on what was then an alfalfa field at the southeast corner of Pecos Road and Val Vista Drive. The parcel of land was owned by the Lund family, who were committed to seeing this piece of land become something of benefit to the booming community. The family's dedication to improving healthcare for the Gilbert community has gone well beyond seeing to it that their land was well developed; the Lund family remains involved in philanthropic activities, allowing Mercy Gilbert Medical Center to cater its service line offerings to the needs of Gilbert residents. In 2006, they committed to a $2.5 million matching grant for building the Lund Family Pediatric and Adolescent Unit in Tower B, scheduled for completion in 2008.

In addition to the Lunds' generosity, the hospital continues to receive generous support from other members of the community. Through the G.I.F.T. Campaign (Gilbert Investing For Tomorrow), the CHW Foundation—East Valley hopes to raise an additional ten million dollars to help Mercy Gilbert increase bed capacity and service lines within the first eighteen months of operation. Significant gifts from the Gila River Indian Community and from Mercy Gilbert employees bring the campaign ever closer to ts goal.

Involving the Community

As the construction process began, Mercy Gilbert set out to get to know the community right away—and to give their neighbors a chance to become a part of Gilbert's history by participating in a handful of community events.

Gilbert Chamber of Commerce

Services Offered to the Community

Residents of Gilbert finally have access to a full array of programs and services, including the following:

- A 33-bay **Emergency Department**
- A 30-bed **Medical and Surgical Unit**
- A 30-bed **Telemetry Unit**
- A 12-bed **Intensive Care Unit**

A state-of-the-art **Radiology Department**, featuring Web-based PACS; digital mammography; 64-slice CT scanner; full-body MRI; digital X-ray machine; cardiac nuclear medicine; diagnostic and therapeutic interventional procedures; vascular procedures; high-resolution ultrasound, and whole-body bone density studies

Heart Center, providing state-of-the-art cardiac ultrasound digital imaging, high-quality electrocardiograms and the most advanced body plethysmography available, and a state-of-the-art digital angiography suite

Family Birthing Center, consisting of six private Labor, Delivery, and Recovery suites, 16 private couplet care rooms, two Cesarean section suites with adjacent recovery room, and nursery. The nursery includes four Special Care beds for infants needing extra care and support.

Laboratory, performing all emergency testing throughout the hospital

Other vital services, such as outpatient services, Perioperative Care, Endoscopy services, Rehabilitation, Health Information Management, Case Management, Clinical Social Work, Palliative Care, and Spiritual Care.

Creating a Healing Environment

Before the hospital doors ever opened to the public, painstaking effort went into planning every last detail of the hospital's environment. It was of utmost importance to create an environment that allows patients to heal. Mercy Gilbert leadership invested in technologies that maximize patient privacy and increase proper medication disbursement. Interiors were designed to look and feel soothing, and a guest bed was added to each of the hospital's eighty-eight private rooms, allowing a loved one to stay with the patient at all times. Every Mercy Gilbert employee was selected based on his or her ability to contribute to a healing environment. All employees went through extensive training to embed the values of Radical Loving Care, as taught by Erie Chapman, into their day-to-day decisions. A mix of hospital services was developed to best fit the needs of the Gilbert community, with every intention of growing and adding services as the community's needs evolve.

In keeping with the CHW mission to provide quality and compassionate care within the system's core values of Dignity, Collaboration, Justice, Stewardship, and Excellence, and with the Sisters of Mercy order's commitment to healing, Mercy Gilbert Medical Center leadership is dedicated to doing all they can to foster wellness of body, mind and spirit.

Mercy Gilbert Medical Center

A member of CHW

DEDICATION OF NEW MERCY GILBERT MEDICAL CENTER

Topping Out: A tradition in the construction industry is to celebrate the placement of the last beam in the frame of the building. Mercy Gilbert did things slightly differently. In July 2005, they topped out the building with a dome-raising event, inviting local leadership to sign the dome that would be placed atop the hospital—a literal topping off of the building.

ENTRANCE

TOPPING OUT

About the Author

Dale Hallock came to Gilbert, Arizona, with his family, who migrated from Anadarko, Oklahoma in 1936. He was sixteen months old at the time his family fled the Dust Bowl and the Great Depression that had decimated Oklahoma. Except for a few years while serving in the United States Navy during the Korean War, and two short stints outside Gilbert, Gilbert has been his lifelong home.

Dale graduated from Gilbert High School in 1952 and attended Arizona State Teachers College, Arizona State University, and Brigham Young University. He was president of the Gilbert Jaycees and the Arizona Jaycees. He served as the chairman of the Gilbert Planning and Zoning Committee before serving as mayor of Gilbert from 1971 to 1976. Dale has had a lifelong desire to gather the history of the people of Gilbert, and this pictorial history is a small portion of his writings on the families that have lived here.

GARAGE